THE CLASSICS OF WESTERN SPIRITUALITY
A Library of the Great Spiritual Masters

President and Publisher
Kevin A. Lynch, C.S.P.

EDITORIAL BOARD

Catherine of Genoa

PURGATION AND PURGATORY
THE SPIRITUAL DIALOGUE

TRANSLATION AND NOTES
BY
SERGE HUGHES
INTRODUCTION
BY
BENEDICT J. GROESCHEL, O.F.M. CAP.

PREFACE
BY
CATHERINE DE HUECK DOHERTY

PAULIST PRESS
NEW YORK • RAMSEY • TORONTO

Cover art:
The artist, Joseph Trepiccione, studied illustration and advertising at Paier School of Art in New Haven, Connecticut, receiving a postgraduate scholarship for further study there. Mr. Trepiccione has taught graphic design and currently works for Thompson Advertising in Windsor, Connecticut in addition to doing free-lance illustration. The cover painting of St. Catherine is an interpretation of her portrait found in the hospital in Pammatone, Genoa, where she served the sick and the poor without pay for 31 years. "I tried to give the portrait a feeling of fluidity by using a combination of opaque watercolors and acrylics," says Mr. Trepiccione of his cover art.

Design: Barbini Pesce & Noble, Inc.

Library of Congress
Catalog Card Number: 79-88123

ISBN: 0-8091-2207-3 (paper)
       0-8091-0285-4 (cloth)

Published by Paulist Press
Editorial Office: 1865 Broadway, New York, N.Y. 10023
Business Office: 545 Island Road, Ramsey, N.J. 07446

Printed and bound
in the United States of America

CONTENTS

Acknowledgments

It is a special joy to acknowledge those who have helped in the preparation of this volume, since the labor itself proved to be a rare pleasure. The editors are especially grateful to Professor John Olin, whose own work first brought Catherine to our attention, and to Roger Sorrentino, a student of von Hügel, whose insistence provided the impetus to delve into his monumental study.

Acknowledgment must be properly given to the Capuchin Friars of Genoa, custodians of the remains of Saint Catherine, especially to Father Victor d'Ghilardi, O.F.M., the provincial, who provided much information.

We are also grateful to John Farina, a graduate student of history, for his expertise on Catherine of Genoa in the American experience. The work would not have been completed without the assistance of Betty Hughes, whose sharp and benevolent criticism will be remembered. We are also very grateful to Charles Pendergast for many suggestions, and to Marion Slocum and Elaine Barone, our typists. The editors wish to go on record that after collaborating on this volume, they remain fast friends.

Author of the Preface

CATHERINE DE HUECK DOHERTY is Director General of Madonna House Apostolate. She was born into a wealthy family in Russia in 1900. At the age of fifteen she married Baron Boris de Hueck, and in 1920 arrived in Canada with her husband and young son as refugees.

Penniless at first, and forced to support her ailing husband, she worked as a maid, salesclerk and laundress until she found work with a lecture bureau. Within a few years she was one of the executives of the company, and again wealthy. But she was haunted by the words of Christ, "Sell all that you have and give to the poor, and come, follow me."

In 1931, after the death of her husband, and after providing for her son's education, she sold all her possessions and went to live with the poor in the slums of Toronto. There she founded the first Friendship House. The intensity of her faith and her sincere love for the poor led many to join her, and several years later she was invited to New York to work in Harlem in an interracial apostolate. In 1943 she married Eddie Doherty, and four years later they founded Madonna House, a spiritual center in Combermere, Ontario. They and 125 others have formed a community life there based on prayer, silence, and the honest love of all who come to them for help.

Author of the Introduction

BENEDICT J. GROESCHEL, a Capuchin Friar, was appointed director of the Office for Spiritual Development of the Archdiocese of New York by Cardinal Cooke in 1974. Prior to that he was Catholic chaplain of The Children's Village, Dobbs Ferry, New York, a residential treatment center for children with emotional problems. He is also director of Trinity Retreat for the Clergy, Larchmont, New York, and of St. Francis House for homeless young men in Brooklyn.

A graduate of the Division of Pastoral Counseling of Iona College, New Rochelle, New York, Fr. Benedict obtained a doctorate in psychology from Teachers College, Columbia University in 1971. He teaches pastoral psychology and ascetical-mystical theology at Iona, Fordham, St. Joseph's Seminary in Yonkers, Maryknoll, and Immaculate Conception Seminary in Huntington, Long Island. Father Benedict has written several articles in the area of pastoral counseling and is preparing a volume on spiritual direction.

Translator and Author of the Notes on the Translation

SERGE HUGHES is presently at work on a companion
volume to his *The Fall and Rise of Modern Italy*. He special-
izes in modern political-intellectual Italian history. These
studies, however, go hand in hand with sustained interests in medieval and Renaissance literature. The translator and author of introductory essays to *The Little Flowers
of St. Francis* and *The Essential Montaigne*, Professor Hughes
is also working on a study and translation of the poetry of
Fra Jacopone da Todi. A member of the editorial board of
Cross Currents since its early years, he has contributed to
that magazine, *Commonweal*, the *Saturday Review of Literature*, and *Thought*, as well as to an anthology of critical
essays, *Sociology and History*. After his doctoral studies at
Princeton University he did post-doctoral work at the
University of Genoa. He has taught at Seton Hall University, St. John's University, and the University of Buffalo,
and is at present Professor of Italian at Hunter College of
the City University of New York.

Preface

A mystic is simply a man or woman in love with God, and the Church is hungry for such people. The Church has brought forth many mystics; one who is unknown but should be known is Catherine of Genoa, a saint beloved of God.

It isn't hard to be a mystic. All we have to do is fall in love with God; the rest will follow. Suddenly the simple law of God, "Love one another as I have loved you," will become part of our being. That is what happened to Catherine of Genoa.

Her life may appear unusual but it need not. Anyone in love with God is afire, whether he or she lives at home, in a poustinia or in the depths of a contemplative monastery. A soul in love with God radiates love. Though mystics are not like other people, they are not aware of their difference. They go about life simply, humbly, easily.

This book is filled with a thousand little examples of how to be spiritual. Catherine was a true mystic, for she came from the mind and heart of God and returned there eternally. People begin to pray vocally and later go on to meditation and contemplation. Eventually they cease to pray because they become prayer itself. Catherine of Genoa was such a person, and if we seek ways to be in

PREFACE

love with God, we can learn by walking in her Christ-like footsteps.

People are often attracted by the extraordinary phenomena surrounding mystics such as levitation, bi-location, and visions. Such phenomena are secondary to loving God and only lead to spiritual disaster for those who pursue them. Because people are so hungry for God, they often seek experiences of God in strange cults. But the mystics of the Church call us to experience God by being in love with him; he is already in love with us.

I call you to read this book slowly, quietly, on your knees. Then it will yield up its fruits.

Catherine De Hueck Doherty

Foreword

This volume, *Catherine of Genoa*, includes *Purgation and Purgatory* and *The Spiritual Dialogue*. The only other work comprising, with these two, the teachings of Catherine is the *Life*. The salient points of the *Life* are all dealt with, however, in *Purgation and Purgatory* and *The Spiritual Dialogue* in a more compelling and concise form.

Catherine (1447-1510) was born into the aristocratic Fieschi family and married into the equally powerful and aristocratic family of Adorno. Ten years after her marriage she underwent a profound religious experience. Her husband Giuliano also experienced a religious conversion, and together they began working at the Pammatone Hospital, the hospital for the sick poor in Genoa. Catherine remained there until her death, serving as its director from 1490-1496. Throughout this period she experienced a series of mystical visions or ecstasies.

The works in this volume can most aptly be referred to as the "teachings" of Catherine. Catherine herself wrote no books. Her "works" were completed by about 1522, about twelve years after her death. Some of the material may have been written down during her lifetime. These works are the works of her friends recounting what they heard from Catherine. It is in this way that they can be called her "teachings."

FOREWORD

Purgation and Purgatory is an account of Catherine's understanding, through revelation and meditation, of the transformation of the self through the love of God. *The Spiritual Dialogue* is in three parts. The first is the story of the voyage of the Soul and the Body, with Self-Love accompanying them as an arbitrator. The second part is primarily a dialogue recounting the struggles of human frailty to assert itself against spirit. The first and second parts are stages in Catherine's spiritual development. The third part dispenses with the allegorical figures and becomes directly biographical. It presents her during her last illness and death. It is an account of her final purgation through the fire of divine love.

INTRODUCTION

THE study of the life and works of the fifteenth-century mystic Saint Catherine of Genoa leads directly to many of the more significant issues of our day. Caterinetta Fieschi Adorna (1447–1510) in her sixty-three years embodied not one but many aspects of Christian life that to people of our times have seemed either conflicting or mutually exclusive.[1] She was a married lay woman, a mystic, a humanitarian, daily immersed in the physical care of the sick and destitute, as well as a tireless contemplative. Motivated and, at times, entirely directed by inner spiritual experience, she was a loyal and dedicated member of the visible Church, subject to its authority even in the most scandalous moment of its history.

Her influence is as varied as her life. As will be seen, she sparked the movement toward reform in its Catholic and Protestant expression.[2] Throughout the last five centuries she has been an inspiration to the most diverse Christians: to the gentle Saint Francis de Sales and the hard-driving Saint Robert Bellarmine; to Fénelon and his adversary Bossuet; to Cardinal Newman, who took inspiration from her for the dreams of Gerontius; and to his severe critic, Cardinal Manning, who wrote the preface to the translation of her *Treatise on Purgatory*.[3] A Roman Catholic saint, she is the inspiration to a host of American Protestant leaders in the nineteenth century, as well as to

1. F. von Hügel, *The Mystical Element in Religion* (in two volumes) (London: James Clarke, 1961), I, p. 97.
2. J. Olin, *From Savonarola to Loyola* (New York: Harper & Row, 1967), p. 17.
3. Von Hügel, *The Mystical Element*, I, p. 89.

1

INTRODUCTION

such important American converts as Isaac Hecker, founder of the Paulists, and Mrs. George Ripley, wife of the transcendendalist founder of Brook Farm and translator of her life.[4] She attracted the attention of von Hügel, a Catholic to the last, and of George Tyrell, who left the Church.

The present preoccupation with charismatic gifts and direct experience of the numinous aspects of psychic life, with life after death, the ultimate destiny of man, are all related to the message of Catherine. At the same time such issues as the care of the poor, the reform and renewal of the Church and of social institutions, the Christian use of capital and privilege, the rights and position of women, all these and more receive impetus and inspiration from the life and doctrine of a rich noblewoman who to the end of her days made herself an effective servant of the poor.

Her Life from Birth to Her Move into the Hospital

Catherine was born in autumn 1447 into the powerful Guelph family of the Fieschi and was baptized in the Genovese Cathedral of San Lorenzo, her parish church. She was the youngest of five children of the former Viceroy of Naples, Giacomo Fieschi, and Francesca di Negro, who belonged to another aristocratic Genovese family. It was predictable that she would be either a contemplative nun like her older sister or one of the married gentlewomen who governed the social life of this rich and prosperous port. It is a characteristic of this complex and varied personality that she became neither but combined in her life the most mutually exclusive aspects of those two predictable vocations. She became a married contemplative whose life outstripped in austerity any rigors of the convent.

---

4. John Farina, "Nineteenth Century Interest in St. Catherine of Genoa" (Unpublished manuscript).

INTRODUCTION

Although of noble family and the descendant of Roberto Fieschi, brother of Pope Innocent IV, she was refused her request to enter the Augustinian convent Santa Maria Delle Grazie when she was thirteen because of her age. That great disappointment was compounded by the death of her father in 1461 and the decision of her oldest brother, Giacomo, to marry her to the aristocrat Giuliano Adorno (a member of a family at bitter enmity with her own), for strictly financial and political motives. Why did Catherine submit to this arrangement, since at the age of thirteen she already had "a gift of prayer" and deported herself with "prudence and zeal"? We do not know. Whatever her motives, she and Guiliano were married in San Lorenzo on January 14, 1463, by her uncle, Bishop Napoleone Fieschi.

There followed for Catherine ten years of loneliness, neglect, and neurotic melancholy. Although described as a singularly beautiful woman, she withdrew from the social life of her class for the first five years of her marriage. This reaction may have been in part caused by her husband's behavior; not only was he wasting his fortune, but he was dissolute and unfaithful to the point of having a mistress and child. After five years of withdrawal, Catherine responded to the urging of her family to become somewhat involved in the social life of Genoa. At the end of this period of moderate involvement, from Christmas 1472 onwards, she was again plunged into total depression.

On March 22, 1473, on the occasion of her Lenten confession, which was reduced to a mere request for a blessing because of her psychological state, she experienced such a sudden and overwhelming love of God and so penetrating an experience of contrition for her sins that she almost collapsed. In her heart she said, "No more world for me! No more sin." She remained at home in seclusion for several days, absorbed in a profound aware-

INTRODUCTION

ness of her own wretchedness and of God's mercy. During this time she experienced a vision of Christ carrying the cross, which moved her to even greater contrition and a passing urge to make a public confession of her sins. This remarkable experience, recorded by Ettore Vernazza in the *Life*, is one of the classic descriptions of an adult conversion in the psychology of religious experience. Von Hügel sums up the conclusion of many students of mysticism when he writes, "If the tests of reality in such things are their persistence and large and rich spiritual applicability and fruitfulness, then something profoundly real and important took place in the soul of that sad and weary woman."[5] His no less distinguished student, Evelyn Underhill, points out that "it is certain that for St. Catherine, as for St. Francis, an utterly new life did, literally, begin at this point. The center of interest was shifted and the field of consciousness was remade."[6]

Catherine's life indeed underwent several radical changes at this time. She entered into an extended period of personal penance and mortification, and of profound prayerful recollections that lasted for about fourteen months. This period should not be confused with an episode of pathological withdrawal, because at this very time she needed to busy herself with walking through the slums of Genoa tending to the poor. During these years, she also had to deal with her husband's bankruptcy, its economic consequences, and her husband's conversion. For the citizens of Genoa, bankruptcy was the ultimate disgrace; but rather than seeing in it a cause for embarrassed withdrawal, Catherine transformed it into a means of complete involvement in the life of her city.

Giuliano had by now squandered so much of his fortune that he had to rent the palace in which they lived

---

5. Von Hügel, *The Mystical Element*, II, p. 29.
6. Evelyn Underhill, *Mysticism* (New York: E. P. Dutton, 1961).

and sell other properties. Although we have no details, he became at this time a humble and sincere convert. He would spend the rest of his days working along with his wife among the sick poor. A Franciscan Tertiary, he agreed to live in a continent marriage. They moved into a humble house near the great Pammatone Hospital with its vast wards of sick poor, the focus of their energies for the rest of their lives. Von Hügel sensibly suggests that at this time Catherine became aware of the existence of Giuliano's former mistress and their child, Thobia. There is in her will incontrovertible evidence of Catherine's constant solicitude for the welfare of this child and her mother who, it appears, eventually entered some kind of religious community or third order.[7] Catherine's acceptance of this child and her forgiveness of her husband goes as much against the attitudes of her culture as does her response to Giuliano's bankruptcy.

After 1474, the *Life* indicates that there was a gradual change in Catherine's life. She became more open, freer and less driven in her personality and in her work. There is a notable decline in the guilt motive of her penitential practices and a suggestion that she does these acts from some inner compulsion she thinks is the Will of God.[8]

She no longer had adamant certitude with respect to God's Will. Now she conceded that an inspiration or an infirmity might or might not be directly a divine inspiration. Years later, in her final illness, she accepted the possibility that her physical sufferings were not supernatural, that she should follow her physician's advice. At times she clung to natural causes as an explanation even when most of the physicians themselves stated that her symptoms were of "supernatural" origin.

The devotional life of Catherine in later years took a

7. Von Hügel, *The Mystical Element*, I, p. 129.
8. Ibid., I, p. 151.

new turn. Her need for confession and her preoccupation with guilt for her sins diminished as her desire to receive the Holy Eucharist increased. In a complete reversal of the discipline of the times, Catherine was permitted to receive Holy Communion daily from May 1474 until her death.[9] The focus of her devotion seems to have been the Eucharistic Presence of Christ and the experience of spiritual nourishment.[10] Another noteworthy fact of her spiritual life was the lack of any human spiritual director or counselor for about twenty-five years. It was not until the end of the century, about 11 years before her death, that she received spiritual direction and assistance from the devoted Dom Cattaneo Marabotto, to whom we owe so many of the details of her life. Prior to this, she was open to receiving assistance from others but was internally instructed and governed by God alone, and felt inspired to follow this unusual and lonely course of action.[11]

Another singular element of her life after her conversion was the ability to endure "great fasts." From a psychological point of view, both these fasts and her attitude toward them are fascinating. Beginning on March 25, 1476, and lasting through the next twenty-three years, Catherine could barely eat during Lent and Advent. She ate heartily up to the day a fast began and immediately after it was over. The fasting did not affect her. Throughout that period, she was as active and bright as usual. This inability to eat troubled her at first. Ignorant as she was of its cause, she suspected that she was deluding herself and would force herself to eat.[12] This invariably produced vomiting, and yet she would make the attempt again and

---

9. Cf. Von Hügel, *The Mystical Element*, I, pp. 113–114.
10. *Vita*, pp. 8–9; Von Hügel, *The Mystical Element*, I, p. 115. (All quotations of the *Vita* use von Hügel's own translation. References to both the Italian text and to von Hügel are given.)
11. *Vita*, p. 116c; von Hügel, *The Mystical Element*, I, p. 117.
12. *Vita*, p. 11c; von Hügel, *The Mystical Element*, II, p. 137.

again. These fasts were not seen as penances since she did not experience any hunger or discomfort from them, and they continued long after she admits that she had lost any glimpse of her past sins or guilt.

The first record of her ecstasies occurs during this period. They lasted several hours, and for their duration, she either walked up and down or lay on the ground with her face in her hands, always in private and always psychologically withdrawn from her environment. When they came to an end, she would at first try to explain to others what she had experienced, but since no one ever understood, she gave up the attempt and kept silent. She would also ignore calls of the curious but would respond immediately to any call of duty or charity.[13]

A Discussion of Mystical Phenomena

Reading these accounts today, some five hundred years later, many questions arise. What is the nature of these extraordinary phenomena? Are they miraculous, parapsychological, or the product of psychopathological states? Since these phenomena continued throughout Catherine's life, and since an adequate sampling of such experiences is found in these first six years of her conversion, it seems best to interrupt the narrative of her life and see how this behavior fits into comprehensible categories drawn by contemporary studies in the psychology of religion. The later events of her life will then be more comprehensible.

In considering mystical phenomena, one must look at the entire life and functioning of the individual, because these occurrences will always be part of the whole pattern. Some four years after her conversion, Catherine

---

13. *Vita*, pp. 15c, 97a; von Hügel, *The Mystical Element*, I, p. 140.

INTRODUCTION

Fieschi Adorna emerged a highly competent and totally dedicated servant of the poor. She became soon after director of the vast Pammatone Hospital now united with the smaller Franciscan dispensary. She acted with more sympathy and warmth to her husband, to the staff, the friars, and the patients of this great charitable institution. She was very close to her married cousin Tommasina Fieschi.[14] Her wills (she wrote several) showed an abiding concern for the welfare of her relatives, especially unmarried nieces, and for her humble servant girls, at least one of whom had some emotional disorder.[15] Later, as an older woman, she would be a close friend of Ettore Vernazza, a deeply spiritual person and even more effective servant of the poor.

Catherine was not a withdrawn and isolated person. But she had an almost overwhelming spiritual sensitivity, a sensitivity so powerful and compelling that a person of less strength and acumen might well have been destroyed. This is why, as has been mentioned, she combined elements in her life that are often mutually exclusive. A solitary, she was surrounded by needful people. Though her inner world was compelling to the point of ecstasy, she responded normally to the outer world. Von Hügel has studied this capacity in his amazingly thorough way and has concluded that she harmonized psychological chaos by "constant and immense effort, a practically unbroken grace-getting and self-giving, an ever-growing heroism and indeed sanctity, and, with and through all of these things, a corresponding expansive and virile joy."[16]

We owe a great deal to von Hügel. Still, while he used the best psychiatric theory available to establish Catherine's basically healthy personality, he was not

---

14. *Vita*, p. 12; von Hügel, *The Mystical Element* I, pp. 131ff.
15. Von Hügel, *The Mystical Element*, I, pp. 311ff.
16. Ibid., I, p. 223.

8

aware of the insights of psychodynamic theory, which was only then developing. Today with the help of these psychodynamic insights it is possible to give a more persuasive account of some of the unusual phenomena of Catherine's life.

There is no evidence to suggest that Catherine Adorna was psychotic. She was a person striving for an adjustment of profound inner forces.[17] Her own doubts about the supernatural origin of her fasts and illnesses, her willingness to listen to others, to be skeptical about the spiritual value of something as dramatic as a forty-day fast, attest to a degree of reality testing inconsistent with any psychotic process. Her ability to relate to antagonistic personalities, including initially her husband's, counterbalances her withdrawal into unusually recollected states. Her ability to rouse herself on a moment's notice for the good of some other person is totally inconsistent with any pathological withdrawal symptoms.

In a penetrating study of the difference between mystical states and schizophrenia, Wapnick has pointed out that whereas pathological states lead the personality to disintegrate, mysticism does the very opposite.[18] The remarkable unity of purpose combined with an ever-growing concern for others and escape from self-centered thinking makes an overwhelming case for the basic mental health of Catherine after her conversion. On the other hand, her depression and the voluntary attempts to overcome this state caused by her loneliness and solitude in the first years of her unhappy marriage suggest a more normal neurotic response to this genuinely miserable situation.

A growing body of theory on the function of uncon-

---

17. Ibid., II, pp. 32–40.
18. Kenneth Wapnick, "Mysticism and Schizophrenia," *Journal of Transpersonal Psychology* 1, no. 2 (1969): pp. 49–67.

INTRODUCTION

scious defense mechanism in the adjustment of neurotic personality, not available to von Hügel, makes this clear. Von Hügel, however, in a very perceptive passage, has an inkling of this fact: "It can be said, in simple truth, that she became a saint because she had to, that she became it, to prevent herself from going to pieces. She literally had to save, and actually did save, the fruitful life of reason and of love, by ceaselessly fighting her immensely sensitive, absolute, and claimful self."[19] In the language of modern psychology, he suggests that some of the phenomena in Catherine's life may be unconscious attempts of the ego to adjust to the overwhelming stimulation of her inner consciousness of the Divine.

For anyone familiar with defense mechanisms, this probability arises: Her penances, grief over her sins, extraordinary fasts, even her zeal for and identification with the poor, functioned as counterweights in her complex personality. This is especially evident in the years immediately following her conversion. Catherine often stated that she was inwardly impelled to do these things and she had a particular distaste for any assignment of merit to what she had done. She never saw herself as the giver but always as the receiver of blessings.

What about other phenomena such as the great fasts that seem to defy explanation? Such unaccountable experiences are so common that it is thoroughly unscientific to claim that they did not occur. Although they are often found in abundance in the lives of deeply spiritual persons with a mystical bent, they are also evident in the lives of persons with no great moral or spiritual acumen. In an often arbitrary way, the phenomena that occur in the lives of otherwise commonplace people are called parapsychological, indicating that they can be related to

---

19. Von Hügel, *The Mystical Element*, I, p. 223.

natural causes not known or understood; those occurring in the lives of extraordinarily devout persons are called paramystical, a term suggesting that they are related to the special gifts of the individual. The fact that in both cases the same phenomenon is observed (for example, extrasensory perception) leads to some confusion. In Catherine's case, the circumstances of her fasts, especially her inability to eat and her complete denial of any penitential character to these fasts, suggests some similarity to the syndrome known as anorexia nervosa. The similarities do not exclude profound differences. Her complete lack of symptoms of malnutrition after a forty-day fast is not compatible with anorexia, nor is her ability to eat heartily immediately after her fast. Thus, we are left with a phenomenon as scientifically unaccountable as a miracle and yet one that bears some resemblance to a psychosomatic symptom. Since these fasts seemed to improve her health and mental functioning, they can in no way be classified as pathological or morbid.

The same is true of the so-called ecstasy. These periods of profound recollection did not interfere with her adjustment to the extramental world. Indeed, she could easily rouse herself if need be. They correspond to profound periods of recollection described by writers as varied as the English philosopher Aldous Huxley[20] and the experimental psychologist Albert Deikman.[21] These states, as both of these writers suggest, may be aids to healthy adjustment rather than pathological states. These profound periods of contemplation then may be seen as furthering a better adjustment. Since, as we shall see, Catherine continued until the very last days of her life to be a highly organized, compassionate, and ever more

20. A. Huxley, *The Perennial Philosophy* (New York: Harper & Row, 1945).
21. A. J. Deikman, "Deautomatization and The Mystic Experience," in *Altered States of Consciousness*, ed. C. Tart (New York: Doubleday, 1972).

INTRODUCTION

available person, this possibility should be considered.

The total dedication to the poor and sick in Catherine presents a more complex problem. Those who are completely driven to the exclusive care of the unfortunate are often motivated by sublimation, a need to express their aggressiveness and egotism in a form that is socially admirable and personally attractive. But frequently, social apostles are motivated by a complex amalgam of motives, ranging from genuine compassion and altruistic concern to sublimation and disguised aggression. If one accepts Jung's point of view, a gradual transformation toward higher motivation may take place in the process of sublimation.

The purity of motive of a person given totally to charitable works as Catherine was can be discerned by two criteria: *consistency*, shown through perseverance in difficulty, a willingness to do the needed task, however inglorious and ego deflating; and *integrity*, or a total integration of the personality into the work at hand. To these two qualities one must add the demand of constant self-criticism for a continual perfecting of motives. This demand cannot be made on most people; when a person, however, appears totally dedicated to a cause, then these criteria conform to his altruism. This is what Leon Bloy meant when he wrote, "You know how much you love God by how you treat thankless beggars."[22]

In Catherine's case we see her gradually growing into her role as servant of the sick poor. Without having planned it at the time of her conversion, she moved out into the city streets. This behavior was not as extraordinary as it might appear in our time, when social service has become a distinct profession. She fitted in with other

22. Raissa Maritain, *Leon Bloy, The Pilgrim of the Absolute* (New York: Pantheon Books, 1947), p. 25.

gentlewomen, "The Ladies of Mercy" who did such work. The great Pammatone Hospital where she lived for the last thirteen years of her life was itself built by a nobleman, Bartolomeo Bosco, as a work of mercy and functioned as a private charitable hospital until it was destroyed by American incendiary bombs in 1944. Thus, Catherine's total dedication to the sick poor was exceptional, but not eccentric.

Throughout the years, Catherine fulfilled all tasks at the Pammatone Hospital from that of humblest volunteer to director. She held the latter post for six years (1490–1496), carrying out her administrative duties with exactness and the same thorough financial care von Hügel discerned in her various wills.[23] This quality of integrity can be observed in her work. She was noted for working "with the most fervent affection and universal solicitude," notwithstanding her interiority, because "she never was without the consciousness of her tender love nor again did she, because of this consciousness, fail in any practical matter concerning the hospital." This consistency and integrity was the result of certain intuitive "rules" that had been given to Catherine in prayer and that it seems are the key to her activity and her consistent spiritual development.

These rules, given early in the *Life*, provide us with the first insight into the unity and diversity of this remarkable life. Catherine attributed these rules to Christ as He spoke to her from within: "Never say 'I will' or 'I will not.' Never say 'mine,' but always say 'our.' " "Never excuse thyself, but always be ready to accuse thyself." These rules are the epitome of that self-criticism which is constantly necessary for spiritual growth. In an even more revealing passage, we read the following about her

---

23. Von Hügel, *The Mystical Element*, I, p. 143.

self-criticism. "At any one moment the love of that moment seems to me to have attained to its greatest possible perfection. But then in the course of time, my spiritual sight having become clearer, I saw that it had many imperfections.... Day by day I can see that motes had been removed, which this Pure Love casts out and eliminates. This work is done by God, and man is not aware of it at the time, and cannot see these imperfections; God indeed continuously allows man to see his momentary operation as though it were without imperfection, whilst all the time He, before whom the heavens are not pure, is not ceasing from removing imperfections from his soul."[24] This evidence reveals the motives behind a life of total yet peaceful dedication, driven, yet not driven in a fanatic sense. Self-criticism dispelled that bitter zeal and querulousness so common among social apostles, even the most admirable. As the narrative of her life continues, we shall see that this growing charity came to flower in the dramatic incidents of the plague and in the moving and affectionate care of friends and humble servant girls.

Continuation of Her Life—
From Her Move to the Hospital
to Her Final Illness

In 1479, Catherine and Giuliano moved into two small rooms in the Pammatone and lived there working without pay and at their own expense. As has been mentioned, she became director (*rettora*) in 1490. During this time, in the early spring of 1493, the plague struck Genoa and raged until the end of August. Four-fifths of those who remained in the city died. Catherine transformed the open space behind the Pammatone into an outdoor hospi-

---

24. *Vita*, pp. 23a and 49a; von Hügel, *The Mystical Element*, I, pp. 138–139.

tal with a huge array of sailcloth tents. She spent months supervising the doctors, nurses, priests, and Franciscan tertiaries who cared for the spiritual and material needs of the dying.

One particular event of this time is a remarkable instance of sublimation. A woman tertiary lay dying of the plague, probably contracted while caring for other victims. In her agony, the woman could not speak. She moved her lips as if to invoke the Divine Name, and Catherine with great compassion kissed the lips of this poor soul tenderly and encouraged her to "call Jesus." As a result, Catherine contracted the fever. She recovered, however, and immediately went back to work. There is no indication in this account that Catherine followed this impulse out of any desire to suffer.[25]

During the plague, Catherine made the acquaintance of a person almost as remarkable as herself. Ettore Vernazza was a wealthy notary and businessman only twenty-three years of age when the plague struck. He threw himself with zeal and courage into the care of the sick and dying, and fell victim to the contagious charity of the woman who would be his spiritual mother, becoming her spiritual son and support as well as the source for much of what we know about her. Ettore himself became the founder of several institutions for the care of the destitute in various parts of Italy, as well as the founder of the Oratory of Divine Love. His entire fortune went for the care of the poor and for the creation of a registry of poor persons in Genoa. Appropriately enough, this closest disciple of Catherine's would himself die serving the sick in the plague of 1524.[26]

---

25. Von Hügel, *The Mystical Element*, I, p. 144.

26. The life and career of this amazing man goes beyond the scope of this introduction but is recommended as recounted by von Hügel (*The Mystical Element*, I, pp. 313–335) as is the life of his daughter, Sister Battista Vernazza (I, pp. 336–366).

Giuliano, Catherine's husband, had been gravely ill since the beginning of the year and died in early fall after Catherine in prayer had been assured of his salvation.[27] Giuliano left his remaining fortune to Catherine to distribute to the poor "to provide the means for her continuing to lead her quiet, peaceful and spiritual mode of life."[28]

During the last year of the fifteenth century, many changes came into Catherine's life. Her great fasts came to an end with the Easter of that year. Now she accepted a spiritual director and confessor in the person of her successor as director of the Pammatone, Don Cattaneo Marabotto. This gentle and devoted man would be her guide and spiritual associate for the remaining eleven years of her life and would provide much of the material for her *Life*. It would seem that this period of almost ten years before her painful illness is what von Hügel calls an "Indian Summer."[29] With a bit more leisure to pray and with the catalyst of spiritual disciples like Ettore and Don Cattaneo, Catherine spoke about her interior life. The driven force of her inner conflicts had been dissipated, and defensive behavior such as the great fasts was no longer necessary to preserve balance. She could relate to disciples and even to a spiritual director. The *Life* contains the following beautiful account of such an interchange.[30] Catherine wished to express some of the great love her heart felt for God but could not do so accurately and so she uttered this mysterious example. "If of that love my heart feels one drop were to fall into Hell, Hell

---

Battista was born to Ettore and his wife, Bartolomea Ricci, on April 15th, 1497, and Catherine was her godmother. Also see footnote: von Hügel, *The Mystical Element*, I, p. 149.

27. *Vita*, p. 123a; von Hügel, *The Mystical Element*, I, p. 150.
28. Von Hügel, *The Mystical Element*, I, p. 152.
29. Ibid., p. 159.
30. *Vita*, pp. 94–95.

itself would altogether turn into Eternal life."[31] Ettore then interpreted this for her approval. She said that the love that united her with God by participation in His goodness was so complete a union that it was the direct opposite of sin, which is rebellion from God. Since this rebellion is the essence of hell and love is the essence of eternal life of the soul, hell would be transformed. Catherine entirely approved of this theological restatement of her intuition but significantly demurred from fulfilling Ettore's request that she pray for her disciples to receive some drop of His love. Her response suggests the perfect abandonment to Divine Will that was the essence of her practical spirituality. "I see this tremendous love to be so full of condescension for these my sons that for them I can ask for nothing of it, and can only present them before His sight." This mode of thinking or doctrine is a further development of her complete acceptance of the divine will expressed in one of her utterances. "We should not wish for anything but what comes to us from moment to moment exercising ourselves nonetheless for good."[32]

These statements epitomized her teaching as she became older and indicate the providential quality of the presence of her two biographers, Vernazza and Marabotto, who were there when her very personal spiritual life could be shared.

During this period of mellowing, several more humanitarian aspects of Catherine's character began to appear, for example, her love of nature and concern for the welfare of animals is mentioned for the first time. She enjoyed walking in the garden and spoke of the being all creatures share as a gift from God.[33] In her carefully drawn and generous will, she was particularly responsive

---

31. Von Hügel, *The Mystical Element*, I, p. 159.
32. *Vita*, pp. 94–95; von Hügel, *The Mystical Element*, I, p. 160.
33. *Vita*, p. 112a; von Hügel, *The Mystical Element*, I, p. 163.

to foundlings and orphans, the needs of her servants and those of Thobia, Giuliano's illegitimate daughter. Although no definite physical illness other than her experience with the plague is ever recorded, it is clear now that her physical constitution began to decline in the last three or four years of her life. She spoke of a desire to die when it would be God's will.[34] In 1509, she began to experience as it were flashes or fires of Divine Love. She apparently spoke of these to her biographers, so there are several descriptions in the *Life* that color all of the writings done later. They refer to her being lost in God, having found her true self in union with life, and to the totally unique world view of the soul in union with God.[35] These experiences, along with Catherine's conversion, were the most important in her life. The more intense mystical experiences were not substantively different from earlier ones, but as von Hügel points out were "as much a gift of herself by herself to God . . . yet her very power and wish and determination to give herself were rendered possible and became actual through that pure prevenient, accompanying and subsequent gift of God."[36]

In December of 1509, Catherine's health began to decline severely. She experienced great cold and interior desolation. During the following months various physicians, including the recently returned court physician of King Henry VII of England, Giovanni Boerio, alternated between treating her as any other and wondering whether her illness was of a supernatural origin. She herself obeyed doctor's orders and never insisted that her illness was supernatural. In late August, she received Extreme Unction and on the twenty-fifth asked that the windows be opened so she could see the sky. As night

---

34. *Vita*, p. 98; von Hügel, *The Mystical Element*, I, p. 183.
35. Cf. von Hügel, *The Mystical Element*, I, pp. 187–188.
36. Von Hügel, *The Mystical Element*, I, p. 190.

came on, she had many candles lit and chanted the "Veni Creator Spiritus" as best she could.[37]

After many physical sufferings, she died at dawn on Sunday, September 15, 1510, surrounded by her friends and disciples.[38] Catherine was buried with some pomp next to one of the walls of the hospital chapel. When the place was damaged because of a water conduit under the wall, the grave was opened eighteen months later and the body was discovered to be perfectly intact without any kind of lesions although the grave cloths were destroyed by dampness.[39] Great crowds flocked to see the spectacle for eight days. After this, the body was placed in the church in a marble sepulchre. The body of Catherine, still very much intact, bears a resemblance to ancient portraits of her. It may be seen in a crystal casket in the Hospital Chapel today. There is no doubt that the preservation of the body very much contributed to the popular cult of Catherine. By popular acclaim, she was called "Blessed" before the Bull of Urban VIII on the canonization of saints restricted this title to those formally declared to be so by the Holy See.[40] Catherine Fieschi Adorna was canonized by Pope Clement XII on May 18, 1733, along with Vincent de Paul, John Francis Regis, and Juliana Falconieri.

Her Teaching

All our knowledge of the life and teaching of Saint Catherine of Genoa comes from three sources, the *Vita*, the *Trattato* (referred to here as *Purgation and Purgatory*), and the *Dialogo*, or the Dialogue Spoken by the Soul, the

---

37. *Vita*, p. 151a, b; von Hügel, *The Mystical Element*, I, p. 205.
38. *Vita*, pp. 160c, 161a; von Hügel, *The Mystical Element*, I, pp. 215–216.
39. *Vita*, pp. 164b, c, 165c; von Hügel, *The Mystical Element*, I, pp. 300ff.
40. Von Hügel, *The Mystical Element*, I, p. 304.

Body, Self-Love, the Spirit, Natural Man and the Lord God (referred to as *The Spiritual Dialogue*). Since not one line of any of these works is known to have been written by Catherine—rather they represent quotations of her spoken words or interpretations—it is perhaps better to call them her teachings rather than her doctrine, which word in English suggests a more ordered and purposeful attempt at a construction of a body of knowledge. Catherine's teaching was simply her own experience of God and of the spiritual life shared sometimes by impulsive exclamation, sometimes as a sharing with close spiritual friends, and in the later years, when she had a recognizable body of disciples, as an attempt to lead others on the way.

All biographies and editions of her work are based on the *Vita e Dottrina* published in Genoa by Jacobo Geneti in 1551 and approved for publication by the Dominican Friar Geronimo of Genoa. This collection was solemnly approved by Pope Innocent XI in 1683.[41] The *Life* is very probably the work of Don Cattaneo Marabotto, her spiritual director, and Ettore Vernazza, her closest disciple. It is mostly composed of sayings, experiences, and teachings of the saint in the form of spiritual counsel. Von Hügel has studied the various redactions, corrections, and editions of this work in a way similar to the exegetical study of Sacred Scripture.[42] However, some of his conclusions must be revised in light of subsequent scholarship, in particular that of Padre Umile Bonzi da Genova.[43] This problem is dealt with at length in the section Notes on the Translation.

---

41. Note: An especially significant fact since it was this same Pope who condemned the writings of the Quietist Michael Molinos in 1687. Cf. von Hügel, *The Mystical Element*, I, p. 253.

42. Von Hügel, *The Mystical Element*, I, pp. 37–46.

43. P. Umile Bonzi, *S. Caterina da Genova* (Marietti, 1961).

INTRODUCTION

Purgation and Purgatory

This work is a collection of sayings and teachings on the general theme of spiritual purgation, both in this life and the next. When read in conjunction with the *Dialogue*, it becomes clear that it is not simply a set of statements on the fate of the saved who are not yet perfectly purified. We read on page 86, "These things that I speak about work within me in secret and with great power." The first redactor of these sayings was probably Vernazza and the first seven chapters made up the original collection.[44] This does not imply that the work fails to reflect Catherine's explicit teaching, even though certain theological glosses were introduced before the official publication in 1551, presented by the Dominican Inquisitors of Genoa who approved the Life.

The Spiritual Dialogue

The reader of *The Spiritual Dialogue* will see that the author's goal is to restate, in more readable and coherent terms than the *Vita*, the inner history of Catherine. One may find it helpful to read *The Dialogue* as a miracle play in which the various figures represent different aspects of the same person. In this way, the characters will pass before the mind symbolically, much the same as William Blake's illustrations for the *Book of Job*, or, in a more modern vein, the characters in Herman Hesse's novels who represent different aspects of the same person.

Part 1 represents Catherine's inner life up to the time of her being made director of the Pammatone Hospital. Part 2 rather explicitly lasts until she "loses her confessor." This incident seems most likely to relate to an

---

44. Von Hügel, *The Mystical Element*, I, p. 91.
* These page numbers refer to this translation.

unusual occurrence of January 10, 1510, when she resolved to discontinue her reliance on Don Marabotto
because he was too indulgent with her. She was already at
this time quite physically ill and had begun to experience
the intense periods of cold that occurred until her death
some eight months later. Part 3 represents an interpretation of the spiritual significance of the last months of
Catherine's life, as well as the unknown author's own
understanding of the highest forms of mystical union to
which the saint had come. It devolves upon the individual
reader to judge for himself how much of this interpretation is based on the writer's understanding of these symptoms (which physicians ultimately considered "supernatural") and how much is a projection of the writer's own
mystical insight. Certainly, the prayers and soliloquy,
especially those on p. 144, suggest that the writer is developing in a rhetorical way what he or she believed was a
valid interpretation of what Catherine had intuitively
perceived long before.

The Characters of the Spiritual Dialogue

It is helpful for the reader of *The Dialogue* to keep in
mind that it was written in various stages and that one
must decide what each character stands for by its own
words.

A useful approach to the interpretation of this text is
one that proceeds along psychoanalytic lines. The Body
seems to resemble Freud's concept of the infantile Id, the
unformed and unrepressed complex of biological drives,
needs, and energies. Human Frailty would appear to be
this Id but already formed and controlled by discipline
and the experiences of life. The complaints of Human
Frailty, almost comic in their pathetic insistence on some
quarter, suggest that, unlike the Body, Human Frailty is
capable of cooperating with the spiritual endeavors of the

INTRODUCTION

Soul. The Soul resembles the Self of contemporary psychology, including elements of the Ego and Superego.
The Spirit, on the other hand, corresponds roughly to
Jung's concept of the numinous or transcendent aspect of
man and since it is not tempted or prone to sin, is also
seen as in the state of grace. The Spirit here also seems to
correspond with the being described as the "Soul" in
Purgation and Purgatory.

Sources of Catherine's Teaching

When considering the sources of Catherine's teaching, one must keep two things in mind. First, she never
studied any source in order to speak or write about it. All
of her teaching appears to be her own spontaneous utterances of beliefs and perceptions that came to her mind as
prayerful meditations or unwilled intuitions, many of an
ecstatic nature.[45]

Second, Catherine was affected by external spiritual
influences, such as reading the Scriptures and other devout works, listening to sermons and instructions, and the
counsel of her confessors and spiritual friends. Perhaps
one of the most potent influences was her cousin and co–
spiritual friend Sister Tommasa Fieschi.

Three specific literary sources are identified by von
Hügel.[46] The first is the Scriptures, especially Isaiah,
Psalms, and the Pauline and Johannine writings. The
second is the explicit use of the poems of praise or Lodi of
the Blessed Jacopone da Todi (1228–1306). This Franciscan friar, a penitent and poet, is best known as the author
of the *Stabat Mater*. An ecstatic poet, and by no means a
systematic theologian, he writes in the tradition of the

45. Note: An excellent discussion of the origin and quality of inner illumination
is to be found in Evelyn Underhill's *Mysticism*, chap. V.
46. Von Hügel, *The Mystical Element*, I, p. 259.

INTRODUCTION

Christian Neoplatonism of Saint Augustine and especially of Dionysius. He would be identified with the reformist elements that began in the Church the century before Catherine's birth and to which almost inadvertently she would contribute.

For some obscure reason, von Hügel overlooks the frequent and conspicuous similarity between the teaching of Augustine on the nature of God and the spiritual life and that of Catherine Adorna. This similarity should be stressed. She herself sought to become an Augustinian nun, as was her spiritual friend, Sr. Tommasa; and there is much of Augustine in Jacopone da Todi.

The third source is a bit more problematic. There is as we have pointed out a very strong flavor of Christian Neoplatonism in Catherine's teachings. It seems most likely that some of this influence would have come from Sister Tommasa Fiesca, who had written a devotional treatise on Dionysius. Marsilio Ficino had published his Latin translation and commentary on *The Mystical Theology and the Divine Names of Dionysius* in 1492 and this work was well known and well circulated. It is likely that this publication prompted Sister Tommasa's work. Von Hügel states that "numerous sayings of Catherine bear so striking a resemblance to passages in these two books of Dionysius that it is difficult to explain them by merely mediate infiltration, and that these sayings ultimately go back to the Areopagite is incontestable."[47] Again, it must be recalled that Catherine was neither a theologian nor a writer. Her use of Christian Neoplatonic ideas was pragmatic, an attempt to find adequate garb for the transcendent experiences she had—a garb that was at hand and more or less fit. Even in those times of great theological controversy, during which her works became popular, the

---

47. Ibid.

24

most strenuous inquisitors did not fail to appreciate this fact.

Furthermore, there is a consistent tendency toward balance and correction of excesses in Catherine's thought. That this balance and adjustment existed in her psychological life we have already seen. In a brilliant analysis, von Hügel[48] lists various Neoplatonic concepts that are expressed by Catherine and then corrected and balanced by the application of some principles from Christian revelation and Catholic dogma. Perhaps the best example of this corrective balance is her apparent identification of her body with the soul's weakness and sinfulness and her idea that sin was the result of the soul's union with the flesh. But these statements belong especially to later periods of her illness, in which situation many people use such expressions. Von Hügel points out that her normal and constant view is that the enemy of the soul is Moral Evil, the self-centeredness of the human personality that constantly tends to make itself the focus of all activity and value judgments.

It is interesting to note that in the great conflict between Human Frailty on the one side and the Soul and Spirit on the other in *The Dialogue*, Human Frailty gradually comes to cooperate in his own demise. Human Frailty says to the Spirit: "Taking into account your resolve, my answer will be brief. I put myself in your hands and hope for a speedy death" (p. 131).

Human Frailty represents the Body in its more mature functioning. The real and permanent enemy of the Soul is portrayed in *The Dialogue* as Self-Love. In a manner that almost painfully captures the essence of psychopathic egocentrism, Self-Love states his case to the Soul (p. 104):"I am not very choosy. . . I am a social being and if

---

48. Ibid., I, pp. 234–237.

25

there is enough to get by for all of us, I am happy. I also manage to put aside enough so that my friends and followers do not lack needed comforts. Indeed I see to it that my friends are very well-off." The character of Self-Love is drawn with great subtlety, blending sensible goals with sensuous ones. Always ambiguous, this character represents the ultimate spiritual enemy of the Soul. In contrast to this total expediency and subtle manipulation is Human Frailty, who having been condemned by the Soul for leading it astray states, "As long as something can be done, I will accept whatever you grant" (p. 128).

Thus, in both the experience of Catherine and in the careful elaborations of her disciplines, nature or the body is not the ultimate foe of the spiritual life. Nature, in fact, is subdued and becomes the servant of the spirit. Self-Love, for which the Soul is responsible—since the Soul alone wills—is the mortal enemy and, consequently, moral evil is not the result of matter but of free human spirit. Catherine is thus led on her spiritual journey not by pleasure but by that happiness which comes from total surrender to God. Pure Platonism is eudaemonist, that is, a natural spirituality in which one is led on by an ever-increasing and more transcendent pleasure of self-fulfillment. Catherine profoundly surpasses this non-Christian philosophy although she also find her ultimate pleasure in the divine contemplation that presents a taste of beautitude in this life. She surpasses this Platonic search by making herself completely subject to the living Personal God. In the words of von Hügel, "The gulf between every kind of Auto-centercism and Theo-centric life, between mere Eudaemonism and Religion, could not be found anywhere more constant and profound."[49]

---

49. Ibid., I, p. 236.

INTRODUCTION

Her Principal Teachings

The insights and teaching of Catherine Adorna may be divided in many ways. For the reader interested in gaining spiritual insights, von Hügel's analysis is certainly comprehensive, but it is almost cumbersome in its exhaustiveness.

For the sake of economy, as well as usefulness, the following four categories may be more practical. (1) God, the Creator of All Life, is Pure Love and the Total Fulfillment of the Rational Soul; (2) The Soul, and the Lifelong Conflict between Self-Love and Pure Love; (3) The Spiritual Combat, in Which the Soul is Only Victorious through the Grace of Pure Love; (4) The Outcome of the Conflict: The Last Things.

1. God, the Creator of All Life, is Pure Love and the Total Fulfillment of the Soul

The profound Augustinian-Platonic vision of God is the bedrock of Catherine's experience. Although Saint Augustine is not specifically mentioned, Catherine's intimate association with the Augustinian nuns as well as the powerful influence of Jacopone da Todi would explain the resemblance between her concept of God as the Living Fountain of Goodness[50] and the identical image in the *Confessions* (IX, 10). God reaches out to the rational soul of man with Pure Love, "As for paradise, God has placed no doors there. Whoever wishes to enter, does so. All-merciful God stands there with His arms open, waiting to receive us into His glory."[51]

The divine motive for this love of God for the soul is expressed in the most often quoted passage of *Purgation*. "All that I have said is as nothing compared to what I feel

---

50. *Vita*, p. 32c; von Hügel, *The Mystical Element*, I.
51. *Purgation*, p.78.

27

within, the witnessed correspondence of love between God and the Soul; for when God sees the soul pure as it was in its origins, He tugs at it with a glance, draws it and binds it to Himself with a fiery love that by itself could annihilate the immortal soul."[52] The motive attributed to God is then Pure Love, which He Himself is and which He perceives in the rational soul—"He [God] did not put Himself in motion for any other reason than His pure love alone, and hence, in the same way as Love itself, for the welfare of the loved soul, does not fail in the accomplishment of anything, so also must the love of the loved soul return to her Lover, with those same forms and modes with which it comes from Him."[53]

This is a highly personalized development of a central New Testament theme in the Johannine and Pauline writings. C. H. Dodd, the New Testament scholar, has pointed out that "although Jesus did not use phrases like 'Thou shalt love God' when speaking His own language, He rather emphasized filial imitation of God's love." Jesus says (in effect) "God is your Father; become what you are, His child. To live as God's child means as a matter of course, trust and obedience. . . . The Child of God will be like his Father, at least to the extent that he will feel himself obliged to try to reproduce in his behavior toward others the quality of God's action toward His children."[54]

Catherine's intense personality took this teaching in the most direct and passionate sense, and hence her teaching, although often expressed in Neoplatonic terms, goes beyond them in her demand for the most personal and unqualified Christian discipleship based on the doctrine of Sonship and in the works of fraternal charity to which she gave herself totally.

---

52. Ibid., p.79.
53. *Vita*, p. 61a; von Hügel, *The Mystical Element*, I, p. 262.
54. C. H. Dodd, *The Founder of Christianity* (New York: Macmillan 1970), p. 64.

INTRODUCTION

2. *The Soul and the Lifelong Conflict between Pure Love and Self Love*

The teachings of Catherine as regards the soul might properly be called her mystical psychology. Her unusual powers of introspection antedate later developments in psychology. These insights, directly and indirectly, led to the classic introspective studies of Saint John of the Cross, Saint Teresa of Avila, and Saint Francis de Sales. But she was also a bridge between these later writers and those of the second middle ages, especially Saint Bonaventure and Jacopone da Todi, who earlier showed considerable insight into psychological processes. In *The Journey of the Soul to God*, Bonaventure demonstrates a keen awareness of the three basic processes of memory, intellect, and will. By introspection he sees these as images of God and evidence of the divine origin of the soul through creation.[55]

The poem of Jacopone da Todi entitled "How the Soul Finds God in All Creatures by Means of the Senses" in many ways poetically parallels the conflict in the *Dialogue* between the Spirit and Human Frailty.[56]

Catherine unquestionably belongs to the great and almost universal tradition of spiritual writers who have a developmental understanding of the spiritual life, that is, those who see it as a way or a process. She is engaged in a journey, a continued struggle for perfection, or, to use her favorite analogy, an endless battle between the false self and the true self. Like all orthodox Christian mystics, she is clear that the struggle is primarily the work of God seen as Pure Love, to which she corresponds by free will. "Every day I feel that motes are being removed, which

---

55. E. Cousins, *Bonaventure* (New York: Paulist Press, 1978).
56. Translated in M. L. Shrady, *Come, South Wind* (New York: Pantheon Books, 1957), p. 61.

INTRODUCTION

this Pure Love casts out . . . all the time God does not cease to remove them."[57]

The doctrine of the two selves is one that is dear to the most spiritual teachers and is expressed in the words of Christ "Whoever wants to save his own life will lose it, but whoever loses his life for My sake will find it" (Matt. 16:25).

Her conception of the true self may at times have caused her censors some problems, but to their credit they did not correct or gloss over her mystical hyperbole. She states several times that "the proper center of everyone is God Himself"; "My Being is God, not by some simple participation but by a true transformation of my Being."[58] One suspects that the reason these startling passages did not bring down charges of pantheism on Catherine is her obvious ethical dualism—her consistent recognition of the distinction between her moral responsibility and freedom to do good or ill and her exalted concept of God within the soul. Seen in this way, God and the Soul are clearly distinct. It is perhaps not inappropriate to suggest to the modern reader that her identification of her true self with God means two things. First, that her ultimate desire and fulfillment is seen as a perfect union of wills, the highest mystical state. This mode of thinking is hardly new to the Christian. It is founded on many Johannine Scriptures and especially the discourse at the Last Supper.[59] Again, we find an echo of certain Christological themes from Saint Augustine, "Christ was made sharer of our mortality, that we might also be partakers in His divinity. We were made partakers in One unto life."[60]

---

57. *Vita*, 49a; von Hügel, *The Mystical Element*, I, p. 267.
58. *Vita*, 36b; von Hügel, *The Mystical Element*, I, p. 265.
59. Cf. John 14:9, 23; 17:23–24.
60. In Psalm CXVIII, Sermon XIX, 6. *Augustine Synthesis*, Trans. Przywara (Sheed & Ward) no. 310.

INTRODUCTION

The second and equally intriguing interpretation of Catherine's identification of the true self with God is the intuitive perception that the inner image of self and of the Divine Being are psychologically the same. This has been suggested by Jung and should not be pressed too far.[61] It is interesting to speculate that Catherine's words relate at least partially to this experience, which is given theological expression by Saint Gregory of Nyssa who was in turn influenced by Dionysius. Gregory writes, "When God made you he imprinted an imitation of the perfection of His own nature upon the structure of your nature, just as one would impress upon wax the outline of an emblem. You must wash away the dirt that has come to cling to your heart like plaster and then your divine beauty will once again shine forth."[62] Perhaps the most revealing statement reflecting the expression of this woman in her personal union with God is "I cannot abide to see the word *for*, and that word *in*, since they denote into my mind a something that can stand between God and myself."[63]

3. The Spiritual Combat, in Which the Soul Is Only Victorious through the Grace of Pure Love

Catherine is an absolute realist about the immensity of this struggle between the false self and the true. In the *Life* she is quoted as making the following perceptive observation: "This self-will is so subtle and so deeply rooted within our own selves, and defends itself with so many reasons, that, when we cannot manage to carry it out in one way, we carry it out in another. We do our own will under many covers (pretexts) of charity, of necessity,

---

61. Cf. *Basic Writings of C. G. Jung* (New York: Modern Library, 1959), part 3.
62. Gregory of Nyssa, *From Glory to Glory*, ed. J. Danielou and H. Musurillo (New York: Scribners, 1961), p. 98.
63. *Vita*, 48b; von Hügel, *The Mystical Element*, I, p. 266.

31

of justice, of perfection."[64] Her doctrine of Pure Love makes it stand out in bright relief against such a description of false love or false self. She states bluntly, "Pure Love loves God without any *for*."[65]

Catherine was a spiritual pragmatist. She had been called to the highest good and she sought it by every means. Quite coherently, she pondered the outcome of this struggle, especially its result if the individual has not completed the work of purification in this life, or, worse, if he had failed totally. This is the point of *Purgation and Purgatory*. Catherine sees the life of the deceased individual as a continuation of this life. Consequently the purgation of the dead is substantively the same road that the devout striver followed in this life, but with certain differences that result from passing through the finality of death. The eschatology of Catherine will be discussed later, but here it is important to note that she saw the road to victory of Pure Love over the false self as a long and painful one, often lasting beyond the death of the body.

The Question of Quietism

The question of quietism or at least an apparent quietism is always raised against the proponents of the doctrine of Pure Love at work in the soul. This charge of quietism when it is unjustly made appears to arise from a lack of appreciation of advanced spiritual insights the proficient person has attained. At one and the same time, the mystic is aware of the necessity of internal and external good works of moral striving as well as of justice and charity toward others. Paradoxically, though, the mystic denies any claim on goodness apart from God. Catherine

---

64. *Vita*, p. 31c; von Hügel, *The Mystical Element*, I, p. 267.
65. *Vita*, p. 109a; von Hügel, *The Mystical Element*, I, p. 268.

frequently reiterates both convictions. "If I do anything that is evil, I do it myself alone, nor can I attribute the blame to the Devil or to any other creature but my own self-will, sensuality, and other such malign movements. I clearly recognize now that all good is in God alone, and that in me, without divine grace, there is nothing but deficiency."[66] She reiterates this in a most nonquietistic way. "It is necessary that we should labor and exercise ourselves, since divine grace does not give life nor render pleasing unto God except that which the soul has worked; and without work on our part grace refuses to save."[67]

One asks if in Catherine's teaching there was one great step, one decision the individual might make that would be the ultimate response to the Pure Love of God. As anyone familiar with the mystics knows, the answer is perfect trust in God. This was the universal response of medieval spirituality and is best referred to in the Parable of Perfect Joy of Saint Francis. It was widely seen as the ultimate expression of spiritual poverty.

Saint Catherine believed that she had been taught this doctrine of perfect trust by divine instruction. "God let her hear internally. 'I do not want thee henceforward to turn thine eyes except toward love; and here I would have thee stay and not move whatever happens to thee or to others, within or without ... he who trusts in me should not doubt about himself.' "[68]

4. The Outcome of the Conflict: The Last Things

It has been noted already that Catherine saw the spiritual journey continuing after death. The two great realities for Catherine, God and the rational human soul, relate dynamically and intimately in this life and continue

---

66. *Vita*, pp. 22b, 25c; von Hügel, *The Mystical Element*, I, p. 265.
67. *Vita*, p. 25c; von Hügel, *The Mystical Element*, I, p. 265.
68. *Vita*, pp. 52c, 53a, 122c; von Hügel, *The Mystical Element*, I, p. 272.

to relate without interruption through death and into the next world. She carefully distinguishes this life from the next by her emphasis on the fact that the "soul is established for good or evil according to its deliberate purpose at the time." She used the saying attributed to God, "Where I shall find you, there I shall judge you," to make this point.[69]

Her teaching on hell is as mysterious as the subject itself. She places the cause of hell entirely on the individual who merits this fate. "It is the will's opposition to the will of God that causes guilt; and as long as this evil will continues, so long does the guilt continue. For those, then, who have departed this life with an evil will there is no remission of guilt, because there can be no change in the will."[70] The punishment of hell is even part of the will of man. "For I see that man by love makes himself one single thing with God and finds there every good. . . . When he is bereft of love, he remains full of as many woes as are the blessings he would have been capable of, had he not been so mad."[71] Catherine also taught that God was incapable of justice without mercy and that in some mysterious way there was an alleviation of eternal punishment that is not gradual but *ab initio*. Catherine taught that "the sweet goodness of God sheds the rays of His mercy even into hell, since He might most justly have given to the souls there a far greater punishment than He has." "At death God exercises His justice yet not without mercy; since even in hell the soul does not suffer as much as it deserves."[72]

The teaching on purgatory is of course Catherine's great contribution to our understanding of eschatology.

---

69. *Vita*, p. 38b; von Hügel, *The Mystical Element*, I, p. 282.
70. *Vita*, p. 172c; von Hügel, *The Mystical Element*, I, p. 282.
71. *Vita*, p. 173b; von Hügel, *The Mystical Element*, I, p. 282.
72. *Vita*, p. 173; von Hügel, *The Mystical Element*, I, p. 283.

INTRODUCTION

The modern reader who may be recovering from negative
reactions to this subject as taught in school will find
Purgation and Purgatory refreshing and consistent with
Catherine's beautiful vision of the Pure Love of God for
the soul. Surprising aspects of this teaching that contrast
sharply with popular misunderstanding are most mean-
ingful. The soul of its own accord enters this purgation to
achieve the purity necessary for union with God. The
individual neither repents of nor rejects this purgatory, or
the past and its errors, or present pain. The state she
describes sounds very much like that perfect trust and
conformity to the divine will one finds in the most advanced spiritual persons in this life. "They are so completely satisfied that He [God] should be doing all that
pleases Him, that they are incapable of thinking of themselves."[73]

Her teaching on the suffering of purgatory is mys-
teriously contradictory. The souls cannot find "the pain
to be in pain" since they are at peace in God's Will, and
yet the opposition remaining in the soul to God's Will is
the occasion of terrible pain.[74]

Purgation is filled with such paradoxes. No one can
tell the grievousness of purgatory, and yet the souls there
have an ever-increasing happiness. Again, we must recall
that *Purgation* teaches us to relate the spiritual journey of
this life to the experiences of the soul after death. These
paradoxes, like many others one encounters in the mystics, are best dealt with in meditation rather than intellec-
tual study. To attempt to resolve them rationally would
cause them to lose the freshness and originality of the
mystics' presentation of them.

For Catherine, these paradoxes were not the products

---

73. *Vita*, p. 170a; von Hügel, *The Mystical Element*, I, p. 286.
74. *Vita*, p. 173c; von Hügel, *The Mystical Element*, I, p. 287.

of rationalization and theory, they were experiences.
They resolved themselves only in the final stages of beati-
tude. The soul, once purified, comes to rest and abides in
God. She says, "Its being is God."[75]

Catherine was fond of the simile of fire's purifying
effect on gold. Child of a merchant city, she uses this
analogy of the blessed soul being twenty-four carats purified in the fire of God.

"Once stripped of all its imperfections, the soul rests
in God, with no characteristics of its own, since its purification is the stripping away of the lower self in us. Our
being is then God. Even if the soul were to remain in the
fire, still it would not consider that a suffering; for those
would be the flames of divine love, of eternal life, such as
the souls of the Blessed enjoy" (*Purgation and Purgatory*, p.
80).

The Influence of Saint Catherine of Genoa

It is difficult to adequately summarize the influence
of Catherine of Genoa, whom Evelyn Underhill identifies
as the only first-rate spiritual genius of her time.[76] She
died in the very decade when religious unity of Western
Europe was to disintegrate and she was destined to affect
both the Catholic and the Protestant world after that
time. The principal aspects of her teaching that would be
influential are the doctrine of the Pure Love of God,
acceptance of the divine will, the teachings on purgatory,
both in this life and in the next. The unusual circumstances of her life would make her all the more significant: that she was a layperson, a married woman, a mystic
totally involved in the care of others and not removed

---

75. *Vita*, p. 178b; von Hügel, *The Mystical Element*, I, p. 273.
76. Underhill, *Mysticism*, p. 467.

from ordinary daily life; that as a good Christian she had experienced a second conversion—these facts would captivate people of the most diverse points of view. In an attempt to give some insight into the impact of Catherine, it is important to consider the influence of her life and the influence of her teaching separately.

The Influence of Her Life:
The Oratory of Divine Love

Catherine's greatest single historical contribution was the establishment of the Oratory of Divine Love. It is strange that von Hügel, who is so intrigued by the personality of Ettore Vernazza, does not discuss the profound effect of the oratory. This remarkable band of laymen and clerics dedicated to the reform of the Church through the spiritual reform of the individual and the care of the poor was founded in Genoa in 1497 by Vernazza.[77] There were other such movements in Italy founded by reform friars like Saint Bernardine of Siena and Blessed Bernardine of Feltre. However, John C. Olin, in his study of the documents of the Catholic Reformation, not only points out that the Genovese oratory owed its particular inspiration to Catherine but that the establishment of the Roman branch of this oratory profoundly affected the life of the whole Church. Olin writes: "Sometime between 1514 and 1517 a branch of this Oratory was established in Rome— an event which Pastor and other historians have singled out as marking the beginning of effective Catholic reform in this troubled age. . . . The influence of this development, merging with that of the Theatines, was significant, and in its ambit are to be found in the 1520's and 30's

---

77. Compagnie du Divine Amour, *Dictionnaire de Spiritualité* (Paris, 1937), pp. 531–533.

many of the major figures in Italy of the Catholic revival. The point of departure remains, however, the Genovese confraternity, whose foundation St. Catherine of Genoa had inspired back in 1497. . . ."[78] Among those whom Olin lists as influenced by the oratory are Saint Cajetan of Thiene and Pope Paul IV (Gian Pietro Carafa), the founders of the Theatine Congregation.

The Influence of Her Teaching

As her *Vita* spread gradually through the world of the sixteenth century, it influenced such figures of this age of reformers as the young Saint Aloysius Gonzaga and probably Saint John of the Cross.[79] The eminent scholar of the works of the great Spanish mystic, J. Baruzi, sees a strong influence of Catherine in the *Dark Night of the Soul*.[80] Saint Francis de Sales enjoyed quoting the life of Saint Catherine and perhaps was introduced to her through the Theatines. His favorite book, *The Spiritual Combat*, had come to him through this congregation and was most probably written by one of its members, Lorenzo Scupoli. The doctrine of Pure Love and total trust in God, so reminiscent of Catherine, is the foundation of this spiritual classic.[81] It is not surprising that since Catherine had influenced the first oratories, she would influence Cardinal de Berulle, founder of the French oratories, and through him Saint Vincent de Paul.[82]

As a young man, Pierre de Berulle had been inspired by Catherine in his *Traite de l'abnegation*, as had Pere

---

78. Olin, *From Savonarola to Loyola*, pp. 16–17. Olin cites Ludwig Pastor, *The History of the Popes from the Close of the Middle Ages* (St. Louis: 1953), vol. X, pp. 388–392.
79. Catherine de Genoa, *Dictionnaire de Spiritualité*, II (Paris, 1937), pp. 322–324.
80. J. Baruzi, *Saint Jean de la Croix et l'Experience Mystique* (Paris: 1924), pp. 142–143.
81. Lorenzo Scupoli, *The Spiritual Combat* (New York: Paulist Press, 1978).
82. Von Hügel, *The Mystical Element*, I, p. 89.

Saint-Jure and his followers in writing *l'Homme religieux*.[83] Catherine influenced Madame Acarie and the French Carmelite movement and was an inspiration to Fénelon and Madame Guyon and also to their severe critic, Bossuet. The correspondence of the entire Quietist Controversy on both sides is peppered with allusions to Saint Catherine.[84]

Her influence in the nineteenth century is remarkable and profound. Perhaps because of the general interest in personalism and introspection so characteristic of nineteenth-century Europe, this Roman Catholic saint, now dead for three hundred years, and then without a universal liturgical feast, became very popular in both Protestant and Catholic circles. No less a philosopher than Frederick von Schlegel, the leader of the German Romantic School, translated the *Dialogue* at the beginning of the century.[85]

In Protestant America, she became the favorite example of the perfect Christian, appealing to the entire spiritual movement that flourished in the mid-nineteenth century. Thomas C. Upham, a protestant who for many years was Professor of Moral Philosophy at Bowdoin College, published *The Life of Catherine Adorna* in 1845.[86] Despite the fact that Catherine was a canonized saint of the Roman Catholic Church, Upham used her life to exemplify Christian perfectionism, which was espoused by many writers of the Congregationalist and Methodist tradition. Upham was impressed by the concept of the second conversion. Evangelical leaders like Professor John Morgan of Oberlin College even called this second conversion the baptism of the Holy Spirit and he refers to Catherine as

---

83. *Dictionnaire de Spiritualité*, p. 322.
84. Ibid.
85. Von Hügel, *The Mystical Element*, I, p. 89.
86. Farina, "Nineteenth Century Interest in St. Catherine".

an example of this experience.[87] Upham saw perfect love, free of all desire except for the Will of God, as the essence of perfection. He identified this love as the same as that spoken of by John Wesley, Archbishop Fénelon, and Catherine of Genoa.[88] Upham was also deeply inspired by the teaching of the mystics in general and Catherine in particular on the reality of the divine union with the soul. Other aspects of Catherine's life appealed to Upham and his readers, namely, her status as a married lay person, her insistence that perfection was as available in the lay state as in the religious, her devotion to the poor, and the realism of her mysticism.[89]

Several articles appearing in Protestant publications at that time were generally favorable. George Peck, editor of the influential *Methodist Quarterly Review*, reviewed Upham's works and his life of Catherine of Genoa with generally positive, if anti-Roman, comment and with a hesitancy toward being drawn into mysticism. The August 1865 issue of *Hours at Home*, a popular religious magazine, carried a substantive article on Catherine Adorna obviously based on Upham's works. The fact that she was a laywoman is seen as particularly significant.[90]

Upham's *Life* also caused Catholics to look more carefully at a saint whom they might have neglected. Isaac Hecker, the founder of the Paulists, wrote the preface to *The Life and Doctrine of St. Catherine of Genoa* in 1874; this translation was substantively done by his recently deceased friend and convert, Mrs. George Ripley, the wife of the founder of Brook Farm.[91] Father Hecker makes passing reference to Upham's works but perhaps it was

---

87. Ibid.
88. Thomas C. Upham, *Life of Catherine Adorna*.
89. Ibid., pp. 16–17, 41, 233–234.
90. Farina, "Nineteenth Century Interest in St. Catherine".
91. *Life and Doctrine of St. Catherine of Genoa* (New York: Christian Press Association Publishing Co., 1896).

precisely this work that attracted him to Catherine. The founder of the Paulists included her statue in the facade of Saint Paul's Church in New York City, where it can be seen today. The great convert priest seized on the popularity of Catherine to correct the misconception of many who honestly fancied that the Catholic Church fostered mechanical piety.[92] Like Upham, he recognized in Catherine one for whom the Holy Spirit and the second conversion were of essential importance. Yet she had been able to integrate this profound personal experience into the life of a faithful Catholic and fervent devotee of the sacraments, especially the Holy Eucharist. This correspondence between the Holy Spirit's work in the soul and in the visible Church was one of the most important themes in Hecker's writings.[93]

An interesting aspect of the nineteenth-century interest in Catherine is related to the recently raised question of women's rights. The Protestant Perfectionist Movement was often involved in the question of women's role in the Church and in society. Phoebe Palmer, who led Upham to an interest in spiritual perfection, was also an advocate of women's rights; and Oberlin College, a center of the Perfectionist Movement, graduated the first women from a school in theology in 1850.[94] To all of these people, Catherine Adorna was both an example of perfection in the lay life and a woman who had filled a position of leadership in the Church and in public charity.

While Americans were being influenced by Catherine, there was a corresponding interest in England, although that interest was decidedly more Anglican and Roman Catholic. The focus of this interest appears to

---

92. Ibid., p. 7.
93. Cf. Isaac Hecker, *The Church and The Age* (New York: Christian Press Association Publishing Co., 1887).
94. Cf. Farina.

have centered on the Catholic teaching on purgatory. Possibly renewed interest in Catholic dogma and the traditions of the ancient and medieval Church gave rise to new interest in the fate of the dead. The Oxford Movement had opened up many areas of belief and theological speculation that had been ignored for a long time. The founders of the Oxford Movement were also deeply interested in the spiritual life. When a host of related questions came to the fore, Catherine's teachings were found to provide many answers. It is significant that the interest in Catherine was focused on three Anglican converts, Manning, Faber, and Newman. Cardinal Manning wrote a preface to the translation of *The Treatise on Purgatory* in 1858.[95] Frederick William Faber, who was a writer with a great popular following, drew deeply on Catherine's doctrine of purgatory in *All for Jesus*.[96] Cardinal Newman incorporated much of Catherine's teaching in his great poetic work *The Dream of Gerontius*.[97] Later Aubrey de Vere published a poetic popularization of *The Treatise on Purgatory*[98] and George Tyrell, who had not at that time left the Church, developed Catherine's teaching on purgatory in his famous book *Hard Sayings*.[99]

CONCLUSION

The reader is now prepared to immerse himself in the vital spirituality of this remarkable woman. The *Dialogue* especially reveals the hidden motivation of this remarkable life and *Purgation and Purgatory* opens a new and startling vision of the love God has for the individual

95. St. Catherine of Genoa, *The Treatise on Purgatory* (London: 1858, 1880).
96. F. W. Faber, *All for Jesus*, IX, sections iii–v.
97. J. H. Newman, *Prose and Poetry*, ed. G. Tillotson (Cambridge: Harvard University Press).
98. Op. Cit.
99. George Tyrell, *Hard Sayings* (London: 1898), pp. 111–130.

human being. Both works enrich the understanding of existence in this world and in the next. Like a golden thread, the doctrine of Pure Love runs through the history of spirituality. It touches the lives of the most influential spiritual leaders and writers in all the great religious traditions. It binds together men and women, clerics and lay persons, the apostles of the Lord and the modern social apostles, in the common human desire to be led only by God. This thread runs throughout the history of the Church and sparkles most brightly against a background of dark confusion and moral decadence as it did in the life of Catherine of Genoa. It provides the spark for the beginning of reform as it did with the Oratory of Divine Love. In times when women were severely limited in what they might do, spirituality provided them with the single expression of preeminence, since Pure Love is open to all who are generous.

That this Pure Love is the same work of grace throughout history is seen in this quotation of the great Moslem celibate woman and mystic Rabi'a of Basra, whose teachings resemble Catherine's in the *Dialogue*, and whose words inspired the prayer of Saint Francis Xavier:

> O God, if I worship thee for fear of Hell, burn me in Hell; and if I worship Thee in hope of Paradise, exclude me from Paradise; but if I worship Thee for they own sake, grudge me not they everlasting beauty.[100]

---

100. Cited in Anne Fremantle, *Woman's Way to God* (New York: St. Martin's Press, 1977), p. 54.

NOTES ON THE
TRANSLATION

THIS translation retains the title *The Spiritual Dialogue*, but changes the equally traditional *Treatise on Purgatory* to *Purgation and Purgatory*.

During the first decades of the Catholic Reformation, and particularly after Leo X's bull of 1530 condemning the Lutheran teaching on purgatory, the advantages of the original title, applied to a self-standing part of the *Life*, were conspicuous: Catherine's teaching could be put to good polemical use. Since then, however, we have had time to reconsider. That work is in no sense a treatise. Composed more than ten years before Leo's encyclical, when the teaching on purgatory was not an issue, this is an account of a revelation, verified by daily experience and meditation, of the meaning of purgation in the here and now as well as in the world to come. The work is Catherine's understanding of God's love for His creatures; and her account of a transformation that, abolishing the old self, calls a new person into being is not in any manner or form systematic analysis. Convinced that no words could express what she saw and experienced, she left it to her closest friends to write down what she spoke about hesitantly. That stance says something of the depth of those misgivings.

The traditional title, thus, is a misnomer. A particularly unfelicitious one. It does violence to the mystic's approach to purgation, implies an approach alien to Catherine. Out of respect for her intentions, then, and for the reader's right to a title that suggests a proper notion of the work, the translator has adjusted a sign that points in the wrong direction.

The problem of *The Spiritual Dialogue* also begins with its title, inherited from the first printed edition published in 1551. In that edition it was quite appropriate, because only the first dialogue was included. The entire work, however, consists of alternating dialogue, meditation and narrative, the concluding section being a long account of the last illness and death of the saint. That story reechoes some of the themes of the first parts, but by and large it is concerned with factual reportage and traditional hagiographic ends—the wonder at the fire that, burning from within, was also visible on the outside; at the spiritual nature of Catherine's illness; at the state of incorruption of her body twelve years after her death.

Such concerns have nothing to do with those of the first two parts of *The Spiritual Dialogue*. The last part of the work, consequently, rounds out and completes the story of Catherine as seen by others. The closing, then, compared to the previous sections, is somewhat extrinsic.

Of the two dialogues, the first is the pearl. Again, though, the term "dialogue" is misleading. This is not a Renaissance humanist dialogue among Body, Soul, and Self-Love in which reason and dialectic lead to impersonal conclusions. It is not a discussion of general philosophic import. An account of a critical turning point in the life of Catherine, the dialogue expresses the resolution of a long confusion that, beginning with a state of sin and indifference and progressing through a period of penitential and ascetical practices, culminates in joy. This section comes to its climax in a meditation on pure love, the theme of *Purgation and Purgatory*.

The second dialogue, which continues in this vein, shows less of the consummate literary skill and insight of the first section. The points made are not succinct; they often repeat those of the first dialogue. Not infrequently they succeed in garbling what was clear the first time around. Body, Soul, and Self-Love disappear and are replaced by *spirito* and *umanità*. In allegorical terms the meaning of *umanità* oscillates. At one moment it stands for humanity, at another human frailty, and on more than one occasion the lower self. The coherence of the term is illusory, and the dilemma is whether to translate it with a phonetic constant or terminological changes that come about with disconcerting abruptness. Mindful of the Yiddish proverb that the mere existence of a problem does not imply a solution, the translator not without some qualms has chosen the phonetic constants and left it to the reader to respond to the frequent and sudden changes of meaning. Lacking the firm clarity of the participants in the first dialogue, this polyvalent term indicates at various times humanity, human frailty, and the lower self, and has accordingly been variously translated. *Spirito*, on the other hand, though occasionally ambiguous, is more consistent in meaning. There are, however, sections in which "the soul" is reintroduced where the term has no connection with the personage of the first dialogue but clearly refers to Catherine. For this reason, though at no place in the original manuscripts is the saint's name used, the translator has taken the liberty of introducing it where necessary for purposes of clarity.

The unity of *The Spiritual Dialogue*, then, is somewhat wobbly; but since the translator was unable to hit on a better title he has limited himself to this caveat. He has also dispensed with the traditional divisions of *Purgation and Purgatory* as well as those of *The Spiritual Dialogue*. These numerous chapter headings with their resumés may well have suited the seventeenth-century reading public for whom they were intended, but it is the translator's conviction that the natural breaks in both works are clearly recognizable and that the absence of chapter headings, indeed, gives more the feel of the original manuscript.

Difficulties attendant upon misleading titles and unnecessary chapter headings, however, appear picayune compared with the problem of the choice of the most reliable text, that most in conformity with the mind of Caterina. For purposes of translation, earlier English versions relied on the first printed edition of these works, published in 1551. In the nineteenth century Thomas Coswell Upham, for example, and the anonymous translator of the 1880 edition of the *Treatise on Purgatory* with a preface by Cardinal Manning, based themselves on that text, as did Helen Douglas Irvine and Charlotte Balfour a generation ago. Subsequent scholarship, and principally the work of Padre Umile Bonzi da Genova, has persuaded the translator that that text is not the best available. Manuscripts D and D*, both reproduced in their entirety in Padre Bonzi's two-volume study *S. Caterina da Genova* (Marietti, 1960–1962), offer an unembellished portrait of the teaching of the saint that is far more trustworthy than that of the 1551 edition or Manuscript A, which von Hügel considered best (and which is also published in its entirety in Padre Bonzi's work). The differences between D and D*, on which manuscripts the present translation is based, are negligible. In the rare instances in which they occur, the more readable version has been preferred.

The question of the history of the manuscripts in its involutions is reminiscent of early medieval Celtic ornament; and since the original manuscript has yet to be found, the conclusions reached will be gauged in terms of plausibility, not of certainties. To start with a definite fact, we may begin with the date of Manuscript A—1548. That date is factually certain and its proximity to Catherine's lifetime did much to convince von Hügel that this was the most reliable text. Manuscript D, by comparison, is substantially later, 1671. What von Hügel did not sufficiently take into consideration, however, were the stylistic differences between Manuscripts D (which he knew as Manuscript C) and A. These differences do not speak well for the primacy of A. Manuscripts written at some remove from a saint's death, it is a well-known fact, tend to fill factual lacunae with imaginary plausibilities and to suppress stories that may not be considered sufficiently edifying. The *Fioretti* illustrate the point. The greater the distance between the death of Francis and the hagiographical accounts, these stories show, the more willing the writer is to embroider them with his powers of imagination or of partisan zeal—for the *Fioretti*, it will be remembered, were written at the height of the polemics between Conventuals and Spirituals. (The analogy is only partial, since Catherine in her wisdom never founded an order.) Now, what von Hügel either failed to notice or preferred to ignore was that Manuscript A, the "early" manuscript, read like a late one, and the "later" D manuscript read like a manuscript closer to the source. The account of the mystic's life in A, for example, begins with a long, detailed history of "Catherineta"; by comparison, the account in Manuscript D is very short. The difference is easy to account for. In the first, Manuscript A, the writer, composing at a distance from the event, goes to some pains to acquaint his readers with the basic facts. In Manuscript D the author is terse and to the point: Everyone knows about Catherine and there is no more point in telling the reader, for example, that the saint was born of an aristocratic Genoese family than there would be in telling American readers today that Nelson Rockefeller comes from a distinguished New York family. Again, in the account of Catherine's request to enter a convent at the age of thirteen, a request that was denied, Manuscript A reports conversations between the Mother Abbess, Catherine, and her confessor that do homage to the author's gifts as a historical novelist but not as a historian. Manuscript D, again terse and to the point, limits the story to its essentials. Of course Fra Paolo da Savona, the author of Manuscript A, is candidly honest about his motive for writing—he is preparing his account for a dying Genoese lady in an attempt to console her with edifying particulars of Catherine's story, and toward this end does not hesitate to make the most of his hortatory powers. Manuscript D, instead, has an altogether different purpose: Copied by Padre Angelo Luigi Giovo, the manuscript was used in the canonization proceedings in 1671. A judge in the Ecclesiastical Tribunal of the Ligurian Province and a historian by training, Padre Giovo has something of the Bollandist in him. He makes his source clear:

> This book of Blessed Catarineta Adorna has been copied from another old manuscript given by Sister [name missing], Rector of the Great Hospital, who says she received it from the sisters of the Madonna delle Grazie. It is extremely probable that it is the manuscript copied by Ettore Vernazza and sent to V. D. Battistina, his daughter. This book, given the age of the paper, the print, the binding and other details, has been judged by experts to belong to that [Catherine's] period.

Von Hügel's notion of the progressive composition of *Purgation and Purgatory* and *The Spiritual Dialogue* disinclined him to take this testimony at face value. But the discovery in 1960 by Padre Onorato da Sesto Ponente of a 1632 copy of Manuscript D* threw the full weight of the evidence in favor of Manuscript D. Like the latter, it included the reference

> It is already ten years that the body continues in this integrity in a marble tomb, on high, in a wooden box, in the church mentioned above.

This would mean that the manuscript from which the newly discovered copy was transcribed was written some twelve years after Catherine's death, since her body was transferred to this tomb two years after her death. The likelihood is that this 1522 manuscript and the Manuscript No. 1 referred to in the records of the canonization proceedings, and since lost, are one and the same. Seventeenth-century experts dated that manuscript to the first decades of the sixteenth century.

In sum, then, Manuscript D, though substantially later than A, is a complete and faithful text derived directly from D*; Manuscript A, which lacks the first part of *The Spiritual Dialogue*, appears to be derived also from D*, but is far less faithful to the original.

If we try to get behind the original Manuscript D*—for that, too, is a transcription of a previous manuscript—we become more conjectural; again, though, conjecture is not without degrees of probability.

Ettore Vernazza, thought to be the transcriber, was one of the closest of Catherine's friends. Twenty-three years old when he first met Catherine, who was then in her sixties, the young man was already a very successful businessman. He was also concerned with doing good in some palpable way—in getting through the eye of the needle. Good Genoese that he was, however, Vernazza did not think of giving away all his money. He made the best possible use of it, wearing himself out in caring for the poor, founding associations and shelters, and ultimately dying a hero's death during the plague amidst the poor he was ministering to. Vernazza, however, did not limit himself to works of charity. Catherine appealed to him for her practical virtues, no doubt, but not for them alone. The life of prayer, the pondering of the meaning of God's love, also drew him. This was the hidden dimension in the visible work of giving help to the poor and the defenseless. Practical works of charity, however, constitute his vocation. Writing, by comparison, did not interest him—and in particular writing about Catherine. *That* was a chore:

> In composing this I have written as I have found. One thing I will tell you, that never did I labor as much over anything I put down on paper.

To judge from a clarification that he asked of Catherine on a theological point—not abstruse but worded somewhat paradoxically—it appears, furthermore, that Vernazza was not at all given to poetical or theological flights—one additional reason for him to have exercised particular caution in recording the teaching of the saint. That lack of imagination, whatever it said of him as a writer, was his forte—and our assurance of his reliability. Still, as one of those closest to Catherine, Vernazza very much sought to keep her presence alive, and this raises a problem: In the transcription of the manuscript, did he limit himself to the work of an amanuensis? Probably not; but the extent to which he editorialized—omitted, inserted, or rearranged material—is undeterminable. "*Nel componere*," we read in the concluding paragraph of Manuscript D, "*ho scritto come io ho ritrovato*." The phrase is not clear. The meaning of *componere* is univocal—to put together, to arrange, as in editing. There is more than one connotation, however, for *ho ritrovato*. It may indicate "as I have found the material." It can also mean "as I have found materials that were dispersed" or "as I have found after meticulous inquiry," or even "as I have found the material to be true"—a process of verification, the sifting out of questionable material. Thus an uncomplicated beginning, "In composing this I have written," concludes with four distinct possibilities of varying degrees of plausibility. This is no small difficulty, and two more may be added to it—the recognizable insertion here and there of theological glosses added at a later time, and the use of the "I" for someone who, we know, did not ever write down her thoughts. Do these considerations, taken all together, weaken the case for the reliability of Vernazza's editorship?

The theological glosses certainly do not. Few in number, they are instantly recognizable by their style, or rather by their lack of it. They carefully spell out—read, reduce to prosaic orthodoxy—the more winged metaphors of Catherine or some of her more intuitively compact utterances.

As for the use of the "I," among those very close to Catherine, some either remembered or jotted down her words more or less literally. Those words were perhaps the very words of the saint or a close approximation. In any case, it was in the memory of a group, not of one person alone, that those utterances were preserved; and if the "I" had been adopted to express anything but the thought of Catherine, it is inconceivable so soon after the saint's death that members of her circle would not have denounced the alteration or falsification.

The question that remains, then, is the weight to be given to the ambiguities in Vernazza's attestation, the impossibility of distinguishing precisely what he copied from what he edited or inserted of his own. Again, as in the case of the glosses and the use of the "I," the difficulties are more apparent than real. Vernazza is reassuring. That businessman's imagination, that closeness to Catherine, virtually guarantees the reliability of the manuscript he was copying. Whoever its author, he (the Italian text consistently uses the masculine ending for "author") had to be someone Vernazza knew, someone he trusted.

Summing up, then. Manuscripts D and D* are more reliable sources than Manuscript A or the text of the first printed edition, which hitherto has been the text used for English translations. Both contain the whole of the "*Opus Catharinianum*"—the *Life*, *Purgation and Purgatory*, and *The Spiritual Dialogue*. All of the works were completed by 1522 or so, that is, about twelve years after Catherine's death. This date is the *terminus ad quem*, that of Vernazza's editing. Since some of the saint's teaching was jotted down then and there by Vernazza—and not by him alone—we may assume that to some undeterminable degree the materials date back to the saint's lifetime.

*　　*　　*

This revision in dates does not call for any substantial change either in the text of *Purgation and Purgatory* or in our understanding of it. The Manuscript A version of this work is more flowery, occasionally verbose—and there the difference ends. This is not the case, however, with *The Spiritual Dialogue*: Here Manuscript A omits entirely the first two sections and opens with:

> How this blessed soul went to bed and of her happy death and of the many wonderful things brought about in that death.

For von Hügel the omission of the first two parts was a confirmation of his overall notion of how the teaching of

Catherine was transmitted, more or less modified, and eventually given permanent form. The process, he believed, was gradual. Originally, he felt, Vernazza had composed the *Life*; at some later time Cattaneo Marabotto, her confessor, had written *Purgation and Purgatory*; and much later, Mother Battistina, the daughter of Ettore Vernazza, had composed *The Spiritual Dialogue*. This attribution, which still has wide currency today, was not in any way challenged, in von Hügel's view, by Manuscript D. That manuscript, he believed, contained later material because it was of a later time. Nor did the argument that only someone with a close and thorough knowledge of the spiritual landscape of the saint could have written that dialogue phase him: There was one person that far removed in time from Catherine who would have known her well enough—the daughter of Ettore Vernazza. That Mother Battistina has acknowledged literary gifts, that she was even known to have written other dialogues, seemed to the English scholar further proof, if more were needed.

The now established primacy in time of Manuscript D* and a closer analysis of Manuscript D show the weaknesses of these conclusions. The missing part of *The Spiritual Dialogue* meant nothing more than that Manuscript A was defective, incomplete. In the much earlier original Manuscript D*, *The Spiritual Dialogue* appears in its entirety. This is a weighty factual objection to von Hügel's reconstruction—and it is not the only one. In his research, Padre Bonzi has unearthed a document that makes von Hügel's position virtually indefensible. Toward the end of Mother Battistina's life her confessor had her draw up for his own use a complete list of all of her works. She complied. In that list—a very long one, for Mother Battistina was prolific—there is no mention of *The Spiritual Dialogue*. To argue that she would have withheld that information from her confessor strains belief.

NOTES ON THE TRANSLATION

The case against Mother Battistina's authorship of *The Spiritual Dialogue*, however, is based on more than factual considerations. There are, in addition, objections of an internal order. The similarities that von Hügel thought he detected between the style of Mother Battistina and the style of *The Spiritual Dialogue* are exaggerated. A sustained comparison of that dialogue with some of Vernazza's daughter's works shows noticeable divergences. Aside from the more Tuscan quality of Battistina's Italian, as a writer Mother Battistina was more expansive, her piety conspicuously Christocentric. She quoted extensively from Scripture and was fond of occasionally intricate exegesis. In brief, she was a very different writer from the author of *The Spiritual Dialogue*.

But if Mother Battistina was not the author of *The Spiritual Dialogue*, who was? We do not know. We can state with assurance, though, that there was more than one author. For the three parts of that dialogue cannot be the work of one and the same author. As we pointed out, the first is in part a dialogue among the Soul, Self-Love, and the Body, in part a monologue in which the references are clearly to stages in Catherine's life; the second, less lively and incisive, is made up also of alternating dialogue and monologue, with Humanity and Spirit as the principal participants; and the third is an account of the last illness and death of Catherine, a brief with excursions into other topics, concluding with attestations as to the incorruptibility of Catherine's body. The differences in tone, in organization, in literary skill, are striking. The first dialogue demands a sense of humor, and exceptional ear for homey and telling arguments, and an intimate knowledge of Catherine's spiritual world. The demands of the second are somewhat less. Humor tends to disappear and in places the dialogue becomes repetitive. The allegory of *umanità*, in particular, is unpredictably fluctuating, as we mentioned previously; and so is that of *spirito*, though to a lesser extent. The third section is the most motley, something of a catchall, in content and in style. The account of Catherine's illness and last agony oscillates between factual prosaism and (though rarely) moments of high poetry. In addition to that reportage, this concluding part touches briefly on the old argument between Body and Soul, the notion of purgation and purgatory, and the doctrine of Pure Love. The author also expresses his conviction that probably Catherine's heart was physically affected by the fiery love of God.

Confronted with three such different works, von Hügel and Padre Bonzi, who disagree on some basic points, concur in positing more than one author. The differences matter, though. For the English scholar the whole of *The Spiritual Dialogue* tells us more of Catherine's circle, whereas for Padre Bonzi it tells us more of Catherine herself. The question of the authorship of the various parts of *The Spiritual Dialogue*, consequently, has to be seen in the light of this fundamental disagreement and not simply in terms of disputed authorship.

But coming back to the question of the authorship of the first dialogue, to whom does Padre Bonzi attribute it if not to Mother Battistina? In a very persuasive interpretation of one of the closing passages in Manuscripts D and D*,

> And he who has seen these works for fifteen years and had a close knowledge of her as well as one of more ordinary relationships is convinced that everything that is written and said about her is as nothing compared to the truth,

the Capuchin scholar persuasively argues that this could well be an indirect reference to a confessor's knowledge of his penitent, and if so, would point to Cattaneo Marabotto, Cathrine's confessor. This reference could not attest to Marabotto's authorship of the last section since both he and Vernazza were absent during Catherine's last agony. That reference, in Fr. Bonzi's view, points to Marabotto as the author of the first and second dialogues. The attribution is plausible up to a point. If Marabotto had the skills to compose the first dialogue it is hard to see how he could have written the second.

The third part, in many respects the least important, may well be the work of B. Angelo Carletti da Civazzo, as Padre Bonzi suggests, or that of Padre Tomaso Doria. In any case, considering the literary value of the piece, it is not clear why champions of one writer or another should vie for attribution of its authorship to their candidates.

As a consequence of this sloping curve in narrative skills and insight, the reader will probably experience increasing fatigue as he turns the pages. How, he may ask himself, did it come to pass that a work that began with such life in it should slope down to such a grey close? Part of the answer lies in a shift of perspective. The concluding part is meant to be documentary and edifying, characteristics of traditional hagiography. That it is documentary is undeniable, but the concern with reporting exactly what happened makes it fall into the repetitive. When everything matters, nothing matters. A slow death, granted, is a hard one. It can almost strip death of dignity. In this sense the account of Catherine's death—save for that deeply moving moment when she seeks to sing the "Veni Creator Spiritus" as she feels death approaching—is all too convincing. A slow death is also exhausting and messy. That it comes to a serene end in Catherine's case is not surprising; but we are not apt to be as deeply moved as her contemporaries with the alternating stages of that death agony or the subsequent discovery of the incorruptibility of her body. That is not the reason we remember Catherine and turn to her.

NOTES ON THE TRANSLATION

It might be well, therefore, in a first encounter with Catherine, to take some radical measures—to read the selections of her work presented in this volume backwards. That is, to start with the third part of *The Spiritual Dialogue*, then go on to what we have referred to as the second dialogue, and then the first, and finally come to *Purgation and Purgatory*. The approach may not be orthodox. It will, however, make Catherine more understandable and her thought progressively more fascinating rather than anticlimactic.

In this way the reader will respond to the dominant chord in Catherine—joy. For just as the dark of the successive stages of that illness is lit up by sudden shafts of childlike wonder and exultation (in the spirit of Francis of Assisi Catherine calls out to death as Sister Death), joy—a singularly arduous one—is the point of *The Spiritual Dialogue*.

Was the joy that of Catherine herself or the literary creation of the author? With respect to the monologues, though we may not have the *verba ipsissima*, there is no doubt that these are the reflections of Catherine, her own account of her spiritual odyssey. The author—be it Marabotto or someone else—listened, pondered, remembered. But what of the parts that are dialogue? Catherine certainly never spoke in dialogue form. We have no record of any comments made on the dialogue as a literary form, Platonic or otherwise, though these were years in which variants of Platonic dialogues enjoyed immense popularity. Was the dialogue, then, the author's choice as the most proper medium for paying homage to Catherine and the most fitting literary genre for her thoughts? And why? We do not know the answer. But among the many possible conjectures one is intriguingly plausible.

Catherine herself found life quite complete with a minimum of literary interests. As a member of the Genoese aristocracy she was given an education proper to her station in life, and no doubt literature had some part in it. To judge from Catherine's temperament, contemporaries probably played little part in that "*infarinatura*," that thin powdering with literature. The exquisite paganism of Poliziano, the sporadic and autumnal Christianity of Lorenzo da Medici, the breezy skepticism and coarse vitality of Pulci, would not have been to her taste. The literary idol of the times though poet of an earlier era, Petrarch, probably meant as little to her: She would not have been charmed by his serpentine love affair with Laura or his togaed humanist prose. Whether or not she read Dante is a matter of conjecture. There are no references to *The Divine Comedy* in *Purgation and Purgatory* or in *The Spiritual Dialogue*. Yet if the reference is wanting, the substance of the thing is palpably there. How could a woman of such intense spirituality not have known, at the very least, the *Purgatorio*?

We do, however, have documentation—quotes from a poet we know meant a great deal to Catherine—and here our conjectures are more solidly based. Jacopone da Todi, in Catherine's time, was far from popular. The belligerent poet-mystic who fought with Boniface VIII and wrestled with God, that gaunt intense figure of the fresco in the Cathedral of Prato as an artist imagined him some three centuries later, was singularly not in the taste of the late fifteenth and early sixteenth centuries. His blunt, total opposition to the theocratic Boniface VIII, which earned him years in prison, seemed anachronistic and futile to an age that, while often deploring the papacy of the times, cynically acquiesced. It was not his political stance, though, that drew Catherine to him, although there is reason to believe that she responded to his defiance. (Politics and the papacy of the time may have been of little concern to Catherine, but she could not have been totally unaware of them. The stories of the political exploits of Cesare Borgia, son of Alexander VI, certainly reached Genoa.) Not the political dimension, however, but the mystical and perhaps the "dialogic" aspect of Jacopone attracted her. At the height of the controversy between the Spirituals and the Conventuals, Jacopone da Todi had addressed Celestine V (Pietro Angelerio del Morrone) in his famous poem *"Que farai, Pier dal Morrone?"* ("What will you do, Pier dal Morrone?"), urging him to hold firm to his sympathies for the Spirituals. Years later, Jacopone, a prisoner of the triumphant Boniface VIII, wryly addressed a poem to himself, asking what profit he himself might draw from the experience—*"Que farai, fra Iacovone?"* This turning in toward himself and stretching outward to God probably had much to do with Catherine's need of the poet. The tumultuous lyrical outbursts of the *Laudi* were one moment of this dialectic, the dialogue poems another.

Did the author of the first dialogue share or at least know of Catherine's love for Jacopone? There is no reason to think otherwise. The saint made no secret of it; and if this is so, it may well be that the joy and humor of that section was reported, not inserted by the author. Those traits were truly Catherine's. Indeed, that somewhat puzzling choice of a dialogue as the medium for speaking of very personal aspects of Catherine's life is far more in keeping with Jacopone's taste than that of the sixteenth-century humanists. Though not poetic, the dialogue has much of the massive simplicity and high spirituality of Jacopone. It also has something more—the mellow sense of humor proper to a deeply ingrained Genoese mistrust of rhetoric, even of art; a mistrust quite in harmony with Catherine's—and Jacopone's—temperament. Thus, in dealing with the problem of the relations between Body and Soul, Catherine's approach was at pole's end from that of another contemporary, Michelangelo. Here in *The Spiritual Dialogue*, the Soul is not a knight *sans peur et sans tache*. Often cocky, amusingly solemn in its assessment of its own strength, this knight is often "full of high sentence, but a bit obtuse." And what of the Body? By no manner or means does it bear a resemblance to the Prince of Darkness. It is far closer to Don Abbondio or Sancho Panza than to Satan. Not infrequently its protests are common sense incarnate. When the Body and Self-Love, that other worldly-wise creature who is also not without his good points, protest that the soul's ascetical intensities will undo them, that they cannot go this way, the honest reader will grant that they have a point.

The young Catherine, a scrupulous, tormented woman suffering from acedia and utter spiritual confusion, could certainly not have written or inspired these pages. Nor could the Catherine of the well-known portrait, the middle-aged woman with fine features and austere countenance. The one Catherine that could have inspired the work would have been the saint of the last period, the mellowed God-seeker joyfully convinced now that she had reached the end of all asceticism, that its rigors were no longer called for. The countenance of the enemies of yesterday, in her look backward, no longer appeared threatening, the features of an Antichrist. From this distance the traits of the defeated enemy were now recognizably more human. At certain points, indeed, they were somewhat comical.

Catherine's Platonism, perhaps, is best understood in this perspective. As Fr. Groeschel points out in his Introduction to this volume, that Platonism was of a peculiar kind. It payed lip service to the revival of Platonic philosophy at that time—that of Marsilio Ficino—but deep down it was a medieval Platonism of sorts, strongly Augustinian. Moreover the vocabulary, as Fr. Groeschel very persuasively argues, can be translated into a more modern idiom—that of the psychological insights of today. But like Platonism of whatever kind, the teaching on the two worlds, the present and the one to come, is not the peculiar characteristic of this dialogue. What singles it out is that sense of humor which culminates in serene joy, a somewhat ironic acceptance of oneself and of all one's limitations, together with an ardent desire to be in God.

In the concluding part of the so-called second dialogue, and with absolutely unconscious humor, the writer observes that God confronted Catherine with one last temptation: He had her become an administrator. Not of a small organization, furthermore, but of one of the largest hospitals in Europe at that time. For those familiar with the demands of administration, that testing will be recognized as no mean trial. In fifteenth- and sixteenth-century Genoa holy administrators were rare. So, Catherine kept the books in order; from all accounts she was the very model of efficiency. Like Abraham, however, she was not hesitant to ask God for modification of what was requested. She asked insistently for additional grace, an increase in love for the poor and the suffering. Without that, she argued, she could not shoulder the work. With that divine help, which permitted her to go beyond compassion, Catherine kissed the sores of syphilitics and, in order to overcome a natural revulsion, ate lice. These are not the typical gestures of saints, much less of holy administrators. There is a wildness to them that in its intensity is reminiscent of her joy, a recklessness reminiscent of the God-lover who at first glance seems to be at the furthest remove from the Genoese aristocrat—Francis of Assisi.

Asceticism, for both, was the high road that led to joy, and for each of them the preference was for the baroque gesture. Catherine's reticent ways should not deceive us. When Francis stripped himself and handed over his clothes, signifying all of his possessions, to his father, it was a very dramatic gesture typical of him; but did Catherine, turning her back on money and politics, the very air her family breathed, do any less? The pendulum in Francis swung high and low, from involvement to detachment, from the craggy heights of Alverna to Africa, where he went to convert the Saladin. Catherine never left the confines of Genoa, but her experience of the tension between the contemplative and the active life was no less fruitful. And in the shattering experience of God the two were manifestly one. The common realization that the love of God was a matter of extremes binds the two saints together, as does their daring in asking to participate in that blinding love that, offering all, asks for nothing in return—the Pure Love of God.

Even in words, Catherine was not so far removed from the spirit of Francis. She could not pour out her soul, as did Francis in the Canticle of Creatures; she was not a poet. But something of that heady hymn is reechoed in one of her utterances. In her almost mousy way, in a tone so low that one strains to make it out, we hear her say, speaking of the after-life, "Our being is then God." The statement may or may not be, in the jargon of the trade, theologically sound. But Francis, like Paul and a host of others, would have immediately recognized its meaning, the image it evoked, the swell and hurl of Caterinetta plunging into God.

This is the Catherine we find in *Purgation and Purgatory* and *The Spiritual Dialogue*. For her we should be well disposed to heed the admonition-confession contained in the preface to the printed edition:

> We therefore ask the kind readers not to become weary finding in this work things that are not well ordered and at times repeated. Not much attention was paid to order and polish, or elegant style. The concern was for that truth and

simplicity with which pious disciples (her confessor and a spiritual son) heard the holy woman speak.

In one respect, though, we will have trouble in clearly making out Catherine's voice, and for this the translator weeps. The key difference between Manuscripts D* and D is that the former is chock full of Genoese expressions, constructions, and rhythms. By comparison, Manuscript D is Tuscan, or at least a very polished Italian. For all of his good intentions the translator acknowledges himself incapable of conveying the swell and fall of the Genoese dialect, that gentle singsong quality, the *cantilena* cadences that no doubt marked Caterina's speech even when she spoke Italian. This is no small loss. Centuries later, that Genoese dialect continues to be the language of intimacy, of that small world which by virtue of its size, perhaps, is easiest to love. It was in this dialect that Caterinetta spoke to Ettore Vernazza, to Marabotto, to God. It is the proper idiom in which to take our leave:

Ma mïa un pò:
A Zena una santa tra i amministratui!
C'u Signiu ne mïa da un garbu
Anche nui?

Just imagine:
In Genoa, a saint among administrators!
Maybe there's a chance
for us, too?

PURGATION AND
PURGATORY

WHILE still in the flesh this blessed soul [Catherine] experienced the fiery love of God, a love that consumed her, cleansing and purifying all, so that once quitted this life she could appear forthwith in God's presence. As she dwelt on this love, the condition of the souls of the faithful in purgatory, where they are cleansed of the remaining rust and stain of sin, became clear to her. She rejoiced in her union with God in this loving purgatory, and so did the souls in purgatory, she realized, who have no choice but to be there, and this because of God's just decree.

These souls cannot think,
"I am here, and justly so because of my sins,"
or "I wish I had never committed such sins
for now I would be in paradise,"
or "That person there is leaving before me,"
or "I will leave before that other one."
They cannot remember the good and evil
in their past nor that of others.
Such is their joy in God's will, in His pleasure,
that they have no concern for themselves
but dwell only on their joy in God's ordinance,
in having Him do what He will.
They see only the goodness of God,
His mercy toward men.
Should they be aware of other good or evil,
theirs would not be perfect charity.
They do not see that their suffering
is due to their sins,

for that awareness would be a want of perfection,
and in purgatory souls cannot sin.
Only once do the souls understand
the reason for their purgatory:
the moment in which they leave this life.
After that moment, that knowledge disappears.
Immersed in charity, incapable of deviating from it,
they can only will or desire pure love.
There is no joy save that in paradise
to be compared to the joy of the souls in purgatory.
This joy increases day by day
because of the way in which the love of God
corresponds to that of the soul,
since the impediment to that love is worn away daily.
This impediment is the rust of sin.
As it is consumed
the soul is more and more open to God's love.
Just as a covered object left out in the sun
cannot be penetrated by the sun's rays, in the same way,
once the covering of the soul is removed,
the soul opens itself fully to the rays of the sun.
The more rust of sin is consumed by fire,
the more the soul responds to that love,
and its joy increases.
Not that all suffering disappears,
but the duration of that suffering diminishes.
The souls in purgatory
do not consider that punishment as suffering
for, content in God's will,
they are one with Him in pure charity.
In contrast to this joy,
this harmony with God's will
also brings about a very great suffering.
Its comprehension is beyond all words or thought.
God's grace, a spark of His light,

has illuminated this for me,
but I cannot express that revelation in words.
That vision, which the Lord granted me,
will never leave me.
I will say of it what I can
and leave the understanding of it
to those for whom God wills it.
The source of all suffering is sin,
either original or actual.
The soul in its creation is pure and simple,
free from all stain,
and endowed with a certain instinct for God.
Original sin weakens that instinct.
Once actual sin weighs down the soul still more,
the distance between the soul and God
becomes greater yet;
and it increases still more
as the soul,
moving even further away from Him, becomes evil.
All goodness
is a participation in God and His love for His creatures.
God loves irrational creatures
and His love provides for them;
in the case of mankind, however,
His love manifests itself in greater or lesser degree
according to the impediments that block His love.
When a soul is close to its first creation,
pure and unstained,
the instinct for beatitude asserts itself
with such impetus and fiery charity
that any impediment becomes unbearable.
The more the soul is aware of that impediment,
the greater its suffering.
The souls in purgatory have no sin in them,
nor is there any impediment between them and God.

CATHERINE OF GENOA

Their only suffering lies in what holds them back,
that instinct which has not as yet
fully manifested itself.
In considering how an impediment
blocks our way to God,
and for what just reasons
the instinct for beatitude is impeded,
the soul feels within it a fire like that of hell,
save that it has no sense of guilt.
Hell is evil will,
and since God does not manifest His goodness there,
the souls in hell
remain in a state of desperately evil will.
The evil lies clearly in the perverse will
that opposes God.
Persevering in its evil will,
the soul continues in its guilt.
And since the will of those in hell
when they departed from this earth was evil,
they cannot be forgiven.
Their will can no longer change.
The passage from life determines the soul,
in good or in evil,
according to the nature of its will,
for it is written, "Ubi te invenero";
that is, at the moment of death,
with a sin-asserting will or a remorseful one.
There is no remission of this judgment,
for the freedom of the will
is no longer reversible after death.
It is fixed at that point.
The souls in hell have infinite blame and suffering;
not as much suffering as they deserve,
but one that is without end.
Those in purgatory simply suffer.

Since they are without fault, for suffering cancelled it,
their suffering is finite
and, as we have said before, is diminished by time.

*   *   *

O wretched state of man,
and all the more so since willful blindness
will not recognize it!
Yet the suffering of the damned is not limitless,
for God's sweet goodness sends his rays there,
even in hell.
He who dies in mortal sin
deserves an infinity of suffering in a time without end;
God's mercy, however, brings it about
that only the time has no limit
but not the intensity of the suffering—that has a limit.
In justice God could have imposed
more suffering than He has.
See the dangers, then, of committing sin with malice,
sin for which man rarely repents!
In not repenting, the fault lingers.
It lasts as long as the will to sin remains,
whether in the present or the future.
The will of the souls in purgatory, by contrast,
is in all respects in conformity with that of God.
That is why God responds to their goodness with His,
thereby cleansing them of actual and original sin.
As for blameworthiness,
those souls are as pure as when God created them,
since in leaving this world they grieved for their sins
and were determined to sin no more.
It is this sorrow over their sins
that makes God forgive them,
so that the only thing remaining in them

is the rust and deformity of sin,
which fire then purifies.
Once completely purified,
having become one with God's will,
these souls, to the extent that God grants them,
see into God.
Joy in God, oneness with Him, is the end of these souls,
an instinct implanted in them at their creation.
No image or metaphor can adequately convey this truth.
One example, however, comes to mind.
Let us imagine
that in the whole world there was but one bread
and that it could satisfy the hunger of all.
Just to look at it would be to nourish oneself.
That bread
is what a healthy man, with an appetite, would seek;
and when he could not find it or eat it,
his hunger would increase indefinitely.
Aware that that bread alone could assuage his hunger,
he would also know
that without it his hunger could never abate.
Such is the hell of the hungry
who, the closer they come to this bread,
the more they are aware that they do not as yet have it.
Their yearning for that bread increases,
because that is their joy.
Were they to know that they would never see the bread,
that would be perfect hell,
the case of the damned souls
who no longer hope to see
the true bread and the true God.
The hungry souls in purgatory, however,
though they do not see as much of the bread
as they would wish,
hope to see it and fully enjoy it one day.

This, then, is their suffering,
the waiting for the bread
that will take away their hunger.
I see also that just as the cleansed soul
can find no rest but in God,
having been created for that,
just so the sinful soul has no proper place for it but hell
—that is the place that God has ordained for it.
At the moment of death, therefore,
the soul goes to its appointed place
with no other guide for it but the nature of its sins;
and—in case of mortal sin—hell is its proper place.
Were the sinful soul not there
where the justice of God wills it,
the soul would be in a still greater hell.
Then it would be out of that divine order
which is a part of God's mercy;
the soul would not be suffering as much as it ought to.
This is why, finding no other place more fitting,
the soul of its own volition
flings itself into its proper place.
So it is with purgatory.
Once separated from the body, the soul,
no longer in that original state of purity,
aware that the impediment it faces
cannot be removed in any other way,
hurls itself into purgatory.
Should the soul find that the assigned place
is not sufficient to remove its impediment,
then it would experience
a hell far worse than purgatory.
In that insufficiency
the soul would see itself cut off from God;
and compared with God's love
the suffering of purgatory is a small matter.

CATHERINE OF GENOA

As for paradise, God has placed no doors there.
Whoever wishes to enter, does so.
All-merciful God stands there with His arms open,
waiting to receive us into His glory.
I also see, however,
that the divine essence is so pure and light-filled
—much more than we can imagine—
that the soul that has but the slightest imperfection
would rather throw itself into a thousand hells
than appear thus before the divine presence.
Tongue cannot express nor heart understand
the full meaning of purgatory,
which the soul willingly accepts as a mercy,
the realization that that suffering is of no importance
compared to the removal of the impediment of sin.
The greatest suffering of the souls in purgatory,
it seems to me, is their awareness
that something in them displeases God,
that they have deliberately
gone against His great goodness.
In a state of grace,
these souls fully grasp the meaning of what blocks them
on their way to God.
This conviction is so strong,
from what I have understood up to this point in life,
that by comparison all words, sentiments, images,
the very idea of justice or truth, seem completely false.
I am more confused than satisfied
with the words I have used to express myself,
but I have found nothing better for what I have felt.
All that I have said
is as nothing compared to what I feel within,
the witnessed correspondence of love
between God and the Soul;
for when God sees the Soul pure as it was in it origins,

He tugs at it with a glance,
draws it and binds it to Himself with a fiery love
that by itself could annihilate the immortal soul.
In so acting, God so transforms the soul in Him
that it knows nothing other than God;
and He continues to draw it up into His fiery love
until He restores it
to that pure state from which it first issued.
As it is being drawn upwards,
the soul feels itself melting
in the fire of that love of its sweet God,
for He will not cease
until He has brought the soul to its perfection.
That is why the soul seeks to cast off
any and all impediments,
so that it can be lifted up to God;
and such impediments
are the cause of the suffering of the souls in purgatory.
Not that those souls dwell on their suffering;
they dwell rather
on the resistance they feel in themselves
against the will of God,
against His intense and pure love bent on nothing
but drawing them up to Him.
And I see rays of lightning
darting from that divine love to the creature,
so intense and fiery as to annihilate not the body alone
but, were it possible, the soul.
These rays purify and then annihilate.
The soul becomes like gold
that becomes purer as it is fired,
all dross being cast out.
This is the effect of fire on material things;
but in this purification,
what is obliterated and cast out

is not the soul, one with God,
but the lesser self.
Having come to the point of twenty-four carats,
gold cannot be purified any further;
and this is what happens to the soul
in the fire of God's love.
All of its imperfections are cast out like dross.
Once stripped of all its imperfections,
the soul rests in God, with no characteristics of its own,
since its purification
is the stripping away of the lower self in us.
Our being is then God.
Even if the soul were to remain in the fire,
still it would not consider that a suffering;
for those would be the flames of divine love,
of eternal life
such as the souls of the blessed enjoy.
Though this fire can be experienced in this life,
I do not believe that God allows such souls
to remain long on earth,
except to show His mighty works.

*   *   *

In its creation the soul was endowed
with all the means necessary for coming to its
perfection,
for living as it ought to,
for not contaminating itself by sin.
Once sullied by sin, original and actual,
it loses those gifts and dies.
It can be brought back to life only by God.
The inclination to evil
still remains in the soul revivified by Baptism,
and unless it is strenuously fought leads back to death.

Afterwards,
God revivifies the soul with a special grace of His.
In no other way could the soul renounce its self-
centeredness
or return to the pristine state of its creation;
and as the soul makes its way to its first state,
its ardor in transforming itself into God is its purgatory,
the passionate instinct to overcome its impediments.
The last stage of love
is that which comes about and does its work without
man's doing.
If man were to be aware of the many hidden flaws in
him
he would despair.
These flaws are burned away in the last stage of love.
God then shows that weakness to man,
so that the soul might see the workings of God,
of that flaming love.
Things man considers perfect
leave much to be desired in the eyes of God,
for all the things of man
that are perfect in appearance
—what he seeks, feels, knows—contaminate him.
If we are to become perfect,
the change must be brought about in us and without us;
that is, the change is to be the work not of man
but of God.
This, the last stage of love,
is the pure and intense love of God alone.
In this transformation,
the action of God in penetrating the soul is so fierce
that it seems to set the body on fire
and to keep it burning until death.
The overwhelming love of God
gives it a joy beyond words.

81

Yet this joy does not do away with one bit of pain
in the suffering of the souls in purgatory.
As the soul grows in its perfection,
so does it suffer more
because of what impedes the final consummation,
the end for which God made it;
so that in purgatory great joy and great suffering
do not exclude one another.
If contrition could purge it,
the soul would turn to it in an instant
and forthwith pay its debt;
and it would do so impetuously,
since it has a clear appreciation
of the meaning of that impediment in its way.
(On His part, God does not forgive one spark of the
debt due
in keeping with His just decree.)
The soul, for its part,
no longer has a choice of its own.
It can seek only what God wills, nor would it want
otherwise;
and that too is in keeping with God's decree.
And if the living were to offer alms
for the benefit of the souls in purgatory,
to shorten the assigned time of their purgation,
still those souls could not turn with affection to watch,
but would leave all things to God,
who is paid as He wishes.
If those souls could, in gratitude, turn their attention,
that would be a self-seeking act
that would distract them
from the contemplation of the divine will—
and that distraction would be hell.
The souls in purgatory
attend to all that God gives them,
in joy and suffering;

nor can they have any further concern for the lesser self
since they have been radically transformed
by the will of God.
What He wills for them is what gives them joy.
Were a soul to appear in the presence of God
with one hour of purgation still due,
that would be to do it great harm.
It would then suffer more
than if it were cast into ten purgatories,
for it could not endure the justice
and pure goodness of God,
nor would it be fitting on the part of God.
That soul, aware that complete satisfaction
was not as yet fully rendered to God,
even if the time lacking
were but the twinkling of an eye,
would prefer to submit to a thousand hells
rather than so appear in God's presence.

*   *   *

Having seen all this in the divine light,
I would want to frighten people, to cry out to each and
every one,
"O wretches who let yourselves be blinded in this world
and make no provision
for this one most important need,
even when you are aware of it!
You seek refuge under the mercy of God,
which you claim to be great—
but do you not see that the great goodness of God
will judge you for having gone against His will?"
His goodness must force us to do what He wills,
not encourage us to commit evil.
His justice will not be wanting
and we must meet its demands.

83

CATHERINE OF GENOA

Do not rely on yourself and say,
"I will confess myself, receive a plenary indulgence,
and with that be cleansed of all my sins."
The confession and contrition that is required for the
plenary indulgence
is such, and so demanding, that were you to realize it
you would tremble in terror,
more fearful of not having that grace
than confident of being able to obtain it.

*   *   *

I see that the sufferings of the souls in purgatory
are endurable because of two considerations.
The first is the willingness to suffer,
the certainty that God has been most merciful to them
in the light of what they deserved
and of what God offers them.
If God's mercy did not temper His justice—
that justice which has been satisfied
with the blood of Jesus Christ—
one sin alone would deserve a thousand eternal hells.
Knowing, therefore, that they suffer justly,
those souls accept the ordinance of God
and would not think of doing otherwise.
The other consideration that sustains those souls
is a certain joy that is never wanting
and that, indeed, increases as they come closer to God.
Their rejoicing is for God's ordinance,
His love and mercy,
into which each soul sees according to his capacity.
These insights are not of the soul's own doing.
They are seen in God, in whom they are more absorbed
than in their own suffering,
for the briefest vision of God
far surpasses any human joy or suffering.

84

And yet that vision,
even when surpassing, does not attenuate in the least
their suffering and their joy.

*   *   *

I see my soul alienated from all spiritual things
that could give it solace and joy.
It has no taste
for the things of the intellect, will, or memory,
and in no manner tends more to one thing
than to another.
Quite still and in a state of siege,
the me within finds itself gradually stripped
of all those things that in spiritual or bodily form
gave it some comfort;
and once the last of them has been removed
the soul, understanding that they were at best
supportive,
turns its back on them completely.
So vehement is the soul's instinct to rid itself
of all that impedes its own perfection
that it would endure hell itself to reach that end.
For that reason the soul tenaciously sets about
casting aside all those things
that could give the inner self specious comfort.
It casts out the least imperfection.
Cutting itself off from all
except those who seem to walk the way of perfection,
the soul concentrates itself,
preferring not to frequent places where those persons
find their pleasure.
With respect to the exterior, the soul, however,
still felt itself beseiged
since the spirit could be of little help to it,
for it could find no place on earth

85

from which it could draw strength
such as would please its human instincts.
Its only comfort was in God,
who did all this out of love and mercy
in order to satisfy His justice;
and the contemplation of this truth gave
the soul contentment and peace.
Nonetheless, the soul
does not leave its prison or seek to do so
until God has done all that is necessary.
Its only pain
would be in being excluded from His ordinance,
which above all things it finds just and merciful.
And she [Catherine] would add:
All this I saw as clearly as if I touched them,
but I cannot find the words to express them.
These things that I speak about work within me
in secret and with great power.
The prison in which I seem to be
is the world, the body its bonds;
and they weigh upon the lesser me within,
which is impeded from making its way to its true end.
To assist it in its weakness,
God's grace has allowed the soul
to participate in His life,
to become one with Him,
in the sharing of His goodness.
Since it is impossible for God to suffer,
the more souls immerse themselves in Him
the more they participate in His joyful Being.
Thus, the pain that remains is for the final
consummation,
the full actualization of the soul.
The more sinless the soul,
the more it knows and enjoys God,
in Whose presence it comes to rest.

He who would rather die than offend God
would still suffer the pangs of death;
he would be sustained, however, by the light of God,
Whom he honors.
Similarly, the soul, no matter how intense its sufferings,
values the ordinance of God above all things,
for He is above and beyond
whatever may be felt or conceived.
Such knowledge does not come through intellect or will,
as I have said. It comes from God, with a rush.
God busies the soul with Himself,
in no matter how slight a way,
and the soul, wrapped up in God,
cannot but be oblivious to all else.

THE SPIRITUAL DIALOGUE

I

ISAW the Body and Soul conversing and arguing with
one another. And the Soul said: God made me to love
and to be happy. I should like, then, to start out on a
voyage to discover what I am drawn to. Come willingly
with me, for you too will share my joy. We shall travel
throughout the world together; if I find what pleases me I
shall enjoy it. You will do the same; and he who finds
more will be most happy.

BODY
Since I am subject to you, I will do as you
   wish;
remember, though, that without me you cannot
   do what you wish.
let us, therefore, understand each other at the
   outset;
in this way we shall have no arguments.
Once I have found what gives me joy, please
   keep your word.
I would not want to hear you grumble,
muttering that you want to go elsewhere
or insisting on looking for what interests you.
To do away with that possibility,
let us invite a third party to come along,
someone to resolve any differences we might
   have
—a just and unselfish person.

SOUL
Very well. Who will the third person be?

CATHERINE OF GENOA

BODY

Self-Love.
He will give the body its due and share the
    body's joys.
He will do the same with you;
and so each of us will have what is meet and
    proper.

SOUL

And if we were to come across food we would
    both enjoy,
what then?

BODY

Then he who can eat more will do so,
provided there is enough for two.
If that is not the case, Self-Love will give to
    each his due.
Considering our naturally different tastes,
    however,
it would be remarkable
if we came across food we both enjoyed.

SOUL

Very well.
I am not afraid of being won over to your
    preferences,
since by nature of the two I am the stronger.

BODY

True, you are the stronger of the two, but I am
    at home here.
There are many things here that I enjoy.
It will be easier for me to convert you to my
    preferences, I think,
than vice versa.

The things that give you joy
are not visible nor do they have any taste.

SOUL

Let us start out, then.
Each of us will have one week to do what he
    will—
as long as we do not offend our Creator,
something I will not do as long as I live.
Should I die—that is, if you have me offend
    God
—I will do all that you ask, be your servant, do
    your will,
take delight in what gives you delight.
Bound each to each,
we shall never again be separated in this world
    or the next,
but be together in good and evil.
Free Will will not loosen this bond.
Should I triumph over you, naturally you
    would act the same.

Agreed on this, the Body and the Soul set out in search of
Self-Love. Having found him, they informed him of what
they had concluded, and Self-Love commented:

SELF-LOVE

I am delighted to join you
and have no doubt that I will feel at home with
    you.
I will indeed give to each his due, and fairly.
Should one of you seek to win me over,
I in turn would favor the other.

The Body and the Soul answered that they would gladly
travel all together and accept his judgment—with the

proviso that no offense be given to God, and should any of them sin the other two would reprove him. The Soul then suggested that they start out and said:

> Let me, since I am the more worthy, start with
> the first week.

BODY
> I accept.
> Act according to reason
> and within those limits that Self-Love approves.

Now the Soul, still free from sin, began by taking thought on its creation, on all the benefits God had given it, on how it had been created for eternal bliss, and how, in worth, it was higher than the choirs of angels. It understood that it was almost divine by nature for, drawn to contemplation of things divine, it wanted to eat its bread with that of the angels. And so the Soul said to itself:

> Just as I am not visible,
> so I want my joy, my food, to be in things
> invisible.
> That is what I was created for,
> and in that I will find rest.
> Spending the first week in contemplation
> and looking down on things below,
> I will make my way up to the heavens.
> No other work interests me
> —let him who finds joy in this do so,
> and may others be patient.

And so for one week the Soul spent his time in contemplation, much to the discomfort of the Body and Self-Love. When the week was up, the Soul said:

I have done my part, now you do yours.
Tell me, how did you find the week?

They answered that it was not to their taste, that not only
did they feel little joy that week, but indeed thought they
were going to die. (They hoped, however, to avenge themselves.) And so the Body said to the Soul:

Come with me.
Now let me show you how many things God has
    done for me.

He showed the Soul the heavens with its ornaments, and
the earth, the sea, the air with its birds, all the kingdoms,
dominions, cities, provinces, spiritual and temporal, great
treasures and songs and music, as well as all sorts of food
for the nourishment of the Body; in a word, all the joys
the Body could experience. These goods would not be
lacking as long as they were in this world, and since they
were created for the Body they could be enjoyed without
offending God. And the Body added:

Though you did not show me your beloved
    country,
I will show you mine.
For unless you share my joy,
I know that I cannot have what I wish.
I remember the agreement—let me remind you
    of it.
If you intended to go
and take residence in your beloved country
and leave me to starve in mine I would die.
The responsibility would be yours,
and so would the offense to God.
Self-Love and I would point that out

Now, and this is an advantage I have over you,
I can enjoy all of these joys and pleasures
as long as I live.
When the end comes,
and should I be saved, as I earnestly wish to be,
I will then go on to enjoy your beloved country.
It is to my advantage, then, that you save your-
    self;
and please do not think
that I seek for anything contrary to God or rea-
    son.
Ask my friend, Self-Love, if that is not so.

And Self-Love answered:

In both instances, your motives and reasons ap-
    pear quite sensible.
In charity, though,
each of you has gone outside the limits of the
    reasonable.
God asks that we love our neighbor as ourselves,
and you, Soul, were so little concerned
with the needs of the Body and of me
that we were in danger of death.
Learn to moderate yourself,
to take into account the needs
of your neighbor, the Body, and me as well—
for I, too, could not live in your beloved country.

Then, turning to the Body, Self-Love added:

As for you, you have shown the Soul many
    superfluous things.
Remember that all that which is superfluous
harms you as much as the Soul,

and that is true even if the Soul may not
    recognize it.
If we live according to our needs
we can live happily together.
If you heed my words I will continue to stay
    with you
and, with discretion, we will share common joys.
Otherwise, I will leave.
If you, the Soul, wish to be helped by the Body,
keep in mind that the Body has its needs;
if you ignore them it will protest.
Meet those needs
and it will be at peace with itself and with you.

The Soul answered:

To attend to the body's needs to such an extent
    gives me pause.
I am afraid that I, too, will begin to find delight
    in them
and, unaware of the danger, will settle for them.
Watching you and the Body
so hungry and so intent on what gives you joy,
I sense that I too will become earthbound.
The goods of the earth
do not lead to an increased taste for spiritual
    things.
(Help me, O God!)

BODY
As far as I am concerned, it seems to me
that Self-Love has spoken very well of our
    respective needs.
We should continue to stay together.

As far as your fears are concerned, remember
that if the things that God created could harm
  the Soul,
He would not have created them.
The will, moreover, is strong.
It has been created such
that it can only be impeded by itself.
God Himself does not coerce it.
This is why it is in your power
to grant or refuse what we ask of you,
and when and where it pleases you.
The reins are in your hands.
Give to each according to his needs
and pay no heed to the grumblers.

SOUL

Tell me, precisely
what are the needs that you claim you cannot
  do without?
I will then provide for them and in that way
no longer be fearful.

BODY

My needs are food, drink, sleep, dress.
That is, to be served in one way or another
so that, in turn, I can serve you.
In attending to your spiritual needs, however,
do not vex me.
When I am disgruntled, I cannot attend to
  those needs.
If God provided so many delightful things for
  me, the Body,
think of what he may have in store for you, the
  immortal Soul!

We can both do homage to God in this
    manner—
and when we have our differences
Self-Love will settle them.

SOUL

Very well.
Since I cannot do otherwise, I will provide for
    your needs.
I am afraid, though, that you are both plotting
    against me.
Your words are so utterly sensible on the
    surface
that they force me to be understanding;
yet, I wonder what you have in mind
when you insist that without me you can do
    nothing.
(Still, if this is a trap, please God, I shall
    escape.)
Let us, then, to the honor of God, go on with
    our voyage.

Now as they went about the world, each attending to his
own affairs, and seeking joy in what was most proper for
him, the Soul took another week for itself. This time,
however, it fared very differently from the first time. Its
companions kept insisting on their needs, broke up the
allotted time into little pieces, and in general brought the
Soul down to their level.

To give up the contemplation of things divine in
order to provide for animal needs greatly upset the Soul.
The difference between its first week and this one, it felt,
was the difference between black and white.

It was then the body's turn to take a week for itself.

Because of the Soul's imposed fasts it was starving. Anticipating other such rigors in the future, the Body thought of fortifying itself. It acted resolutely and all the more so since the Soul, incapable of achieving the freedom of its first week, was adapting itself to the needs of the others. So whereas the Soul had had half a week for its needs, which had become weaker, the Body had a full week for itself.

The Soul then said to Self-Love:

> In meeting your needs,
> I notice that bit by bit my own convictions are
>   weakening.
> Are you not getting more than your due?
> And in following you am I not going to be badly
>   hurt?
> Indeed not I alone, but all three of us?
> You are the arbiter. What do you think?

Self-Love answered:

> It is because you were aiming so unreasonably
>   high
> that you feel as if you are debasing yourself
> to come down to our level.
> With time, though, you will learn to moderate
>   yourself,
> to be more sensible.
> Our company is not so bad as you seem to think
>   at this point.
> Fear not, God will provide.
> You are to love God fully, not in this world but
>   in the next.

Take what you can get, and on the best available
 terms.

SOUL

I see now that I have no defense against the
 two of you.
You are at home in the world.
Of what use is my week to me when you so
 insist on your needs
that there is no room for mine?
When it is your turn you want your week free
 and clear;
but when my turn comes up,
you find a thousand things to object to.
Since I can only get the worst of this
 arrangement,
I think it better to give up the idea of
 individual weeks.
Let each one of us find what is to his taste
and live there where he is happiest.
I will deal as courteously as I can with you, of
 course,
for I know how to do no other.

Content with the suggestion, the two accepted the pro-
posal, saying to the Soul: Now each of us can live in
peace, since you have recognized your errors.
 And so once more they went about the world, one
finding some things that gave him joy, the other doing the
same. But the Body, moving around in his own country,
found more and more things he considered necessary.
Each day those appetites increased. The more the Body
and Self-Love, especially the latter, insisted on them, the

more the three became inseparable. All things seemed equally necessary and reasonable. If the Soul occasionally hesitated, the other two protested that they were being wronged; so that gradually the Soul found itself adrift on the limitless sea of earthly goods. Worldly pleasures and joys were all they would talk about. If the Soul happened to think of spiritual things and allude to them, it met with such criticism that it quickly ceased doing so and said to itself unhappily:

If I keep accompanying the Body and Self-Love, how will I ever escape them?
In the name of their needs,
they will do whatever they wish with me.

Nonetheless, intent on not yielding to melancholy and nostalgia for the goods for which it was created, the Soul sought peace and joy where it could. And listing with the wind, it said:

The beauty and goodness and joy of created things
are means for knowing and enjoying things divine.

(Once it had tasted those joys, however, it asked itself:

And yet, what must heavenly things be like?)

As the days passed, however, the Soul lost more and more of its instinct for things divine. It too, like the Body, found satisfaction in the food of pigs and animals. All three were getting along magnificently together.

Now as they fared forth all happy and united, with not one word of dissent, you can well imagine what became of higher reason! No one spoke of it; their concern was all for terrestrial goods. Spiritual matters had become so distasteful to them that they no longer spoke or wished to hear of them out of fear that that might mar their joy. Only occasionally did the Soul feel a slight bent for other joys and that occurred usually with thoughts of death. Once the fear of death was gone, however, so was that occasional prompting.

There was only one drawback to their situation: Although all three satisfied their appetites as best they could, still they ran into difficulties. Because of its capacity for the infinite, the Soul could not satisfy itself with earthly things; and the more it strained to do so, the further it moved away from the peace and rest that is God. Nonetheless, the Soul, blinded by terrestrial joys, continued to try to satiate itself, to find the rest it sought. Nowhere on earth did it find what it sought and that impossibility was the ordinance of God. (Were man to find peace on earth, few souls would be saved. The Soul would transform itself into earth and there would rest.)

And because the Body is united to the Soul, that Soul which terrestrial things do not fully satisfy, the Body cannot give the Soul as much joy as it would wish to. Unlike the Body, the Soul, once its needs are met, remains dissatisfied. The Body's needs, on the other hand, can be satisfied but its appetites are constantly renewed because, unlike the Soul, the capacity of the Body is for finite things.

Both Body and Soul, therefore, were in distress. The Soul because its instinct for infinite joy was hampered by being forced into a vase that was so small that it easily overflowed. The Body, for its part, acted as if creation itself were not big enough to satisfy its appetites. It smarted under the protests of the Soul; and the more it strained to satiate itself, the less it succeeded.

The Soul, as a consequence, said to Self-Love:

Do you see how badly off we both are?
In having me yield to your appetites
you have made me quite sick,
and nowhere—neither on earth nor in heaven—
can I find the food I need.
And how do you fare? What should we do?

SELF-LOVE
You are indeed unhappy, both of you.
I think, though, that we should press on.
We may yet find some food good for all of us.
As for me, I need more than the Body.
Even if I cannot have my fill, at one sitting
I can eat what the Body would consider
   sufficient for a year.
What, then, must your problem be,
you whose capacity goes so far beyond mine!
If we come across food that will satisfy us
more than that which we have found up to this
   point,
we will let the Body have what is its due;
and if it wants to complain, let it complain.

SOUL
But how can we come across food good for the
   two of us?
Is your food celestial or terrestrial?

SELF-LOVE
I am not very choosy. One or the other will do.
The important thing

104

is that we do not return to where you started
   your first week.
I feel fine anywhere else.
I am a social being
and if there is enough to get by for all of us, I
   am happy.
I manage to put aside enough
so that my friends and followers
do not lack needed comforts.
Indeed, I see to it that my friends are very
   well-off.

SOUL

Yet I know that in this world
there is no food that appeals equally to the two
   of us.
We left heaven, where my food is found, very
   far behind.
Will I ever find my way back to it?
The day that we satisfied ourselves with
   worldly pleasures,
God closed those doors to us,
leaving us at the mercy of our appetites.
Confused and virtually desperate, we turn to
   Him now
because of the use we can make of Him
rather than out of pure charity as He would
   rather have us do.
When I consider what I have lost in following
   you,
I almost despair.
I justly deserve to be despised by God,
by you, by hell, and by the world.
In following you, who I thought could help me
   in my needs,
I have become a thing of this world.

I have never found the peace I sought,
though possessing all that I asked for on earth;
and all your appetites and joys heightened my
    restlessness.
Still, I persisted in my confusion,
hoping in a worldly future that would satisfy
    my craving.
In acceding to the desires of the Body, under
    the guise of necessity
—a notion that led straightaway to that of the
    necessity of the superfluous—
in a very short time I became enmeshed in sin.
I became arid and heavy, a thing of the earth.
The appetites and food of the Body and of Self-
    Love were mine;
and you, Self-Love,
had so tightly bound yourself to me and the
    Body
that I almost suffocated.
In my blindness the only good left to me,
    remorse, did not work in me long.
I continued to lose myself in things that gave
    me shame,
and as I moved further and further away from
    God,
my unhappiness grew proportionately.
I sighed with longing, not knowing what it was
    I sought—
and that was the prompting, the instinct for
    God,
that was mine by nature.
God, who is all good, does not abandon His
    creatures.
He often sends them a sign or a word
that, if man pays heed, will help him,
and if he refuses his condition will be worse yet.

Thus, in my ingratitude I deepened my sin,
taking pleasure in it and even boasting of it.
The more grace I received,
the more blinded and desperate I became.
Had God not come to my aid I would have
   perished.
Wretched me, who is to save me but God
   alone?

Thus, after allowing the Soul to exhaust itself in a vain quest, God illumined it. The Soul realized its errors, the dangers it had fallen into, and that God alone could free it. Fully conscious at this point of the spiritual and bodily death confronting it, of having become like an animal willingly led to slaughter, the Soul was overcome with fright. Turning to God as best it could it said:

Domine fac ut videam lumen,
so that I may escape the snares of my enemies.

The Soul placed all its trust in God, let Him do what He would. From this time on, the Soul said:

I consider all that befalls me, except sin,
as coming from the hand of God.
Sin is mine alone just as is all concern with the
   self.

On seeing the creature lose all confidence in itself and turn to Him, God comes to his aid. He is ready to knock at the door of the Soul, and when it is opened to Him He enters within and casts out all his enemies and restores to His creature its original innocence. He does this in diverse ways, as He sees fit. In this instance we will speak of how He does so with Pure Love.

*   *   *

God illumines us with that love which has no need of us and which sustains us even though many of us, considering our inclination to evil, may rightfully be considered his enemies. Our sins, as long as we are in this world, do not ever make Him so wrathful that He ceases to do us good. Indeed, the more distance our sins put between us and God, the more insistent His call to us not to turn our backs on Him. He loves us and will not ever leave off doing us good. He does so in so many ways that the creature may well ask: Who am I that God has no concern but me?

God shows the creature that Pure Love in which He created it, the same love that brought into being the angels and Adam, a pure and intense love with which He wishes to be loved.

(In making the creature subject to Him, God assured that man, given the excellence of his body and soul, might not consider himself God; that is why He gave man a sense of dependence.)

This love pointed to the greater good yet for which man was created: the return, body and soul, of the creature to his celestial home.

After this, God had the creature realize the wretchedness of sin, against which there was no defense save the love of God. He also showed the creature in a short-lived vision the flaming love of Christ, from His incarnation to His ascension, His work in freeing us from eternal damnation, and how the soul of man was free and subject to God.

God also showed the creature how patiently His love waited, how He abhorred many sins; for had the soul died then and there it would have been perpetually damned.

Her soul, he showed her, had come close to death. He alone in the gentlest of ways had saved her, acting on her with such tender affection that she was virtually forced to do His will.

For God is terrible only in dealing with sin, since in His presence there cannot be the slightest stain. Sin and sin alone is the object of God's hatred, for it prevents His love from transforming us.

In this life, but not in its aftermath, that flaming love never ceases, no matter what the sins of man. That merciful love, Catherine saw, penetrates as deep as hell. Although man merits limitless pain in an infinite time, God's mercy puts a limit not to the time but to the suffering.

In this world, the rays of God's love, unbeknownst to man, encircle man all about, hungrily seeking to penetrate him. When barred, when the soul damns itself, it is almost as if that voice were to say, "Such is the love I bear this soul that I would never wish to leave it."

Once the soul is emptied of love, however, it becomes as evil as love is gentle. I say almost, for God still shows it some mercy.

*   *   *

This soul [Catherine] witnessed many other signs of God's love that are beyond telling.

A ray of God's love wounded her heart, making her soul experience a flaming love arising from the divine fount. At that instant, she was outside of herself, beyond intellect, tongue, or feeling. Fixed in that pure and divine love, henceforth she never ceased to dwell on it.

She was also made to understand the extent of her ingratitude and mirrored herself in her sins; and she was overcome with such despair and self-loathing that she was tempted to publicly confess her sins. And Catherine's soul cried out, "O Lord, no more world, no more sins!"

She did not view sins principally as sins but as offenses against the goodness of God, His strong love. It was the consciousness of that that made her turn against herself, and do her utmost to translate that love into deeds.

In this resolve, the ray of God so united her to Him that from this time on no force or passion could separate them from one another. In witness of this union, some three days later, when she had not yet confessed, she felt the pull of Holy Communion, which from that day on never left her. No priest or friar objected to this need, the daily reception of the Blessed Sacrament, for such was the will of God.

Having witnessed these many signs of the intensity and purity of God's love, the Soul paused and said to the Body and to Self-Love:

> My brothers, God has manifested to me the truth
>   of His love.
> Now I am no longer principally concerned
> with you or your needs, much less your words.
> Had I listened to you I would be lost.
> Had I not experienced it, I would never have
>   believed
> that under the guise of the good and the
>   necessary
> you led me to the brink of eternal death.
> And so I will now do to you what you did to me.
> I no longer have any human respect for you.
> You are my mortal enemies,
> and I will have no further dealings with you.
> Like the damned, lose all hope.
> I will make every effort to return to that life
> from which I started out,
> the one from which, through pretense, you had
>   me turn away.
> With God's help I will no longer be deceived by
>   you.

Still, I hope to act in such a way
that each will have what is due him.
As you made me do what I should not have done,
so I will have you do what you would rather not
    do.
In this way, you may satisfy the spirit.
I hope to subject you completely to me—
that is, have you go against your natural bent.

On sensing that resolve in the Soul and realizing that the
Soul had indeed been illumined, the Body and Self-Love,
who could no longer deceive the Soul, were extremely
distressed.

We are subject to you
They said—

Be just and do with us what you will.
If we cannot get by any other way, we will steal;
that is, you will do all you can against us
and we will repay you in kind.
In the end, each will get his due.

The Soul answered:

Let me offer you a consoling truth.
Now you are sore distressed,
but once you free yourself of superfluous things,
then you will rejoice in everything I have said
    and done.
You will share my good forever.
Be at peace, then, for in the end we shall enjoy
    the peace of God.
I will not fail to provide, moreover, for your just
    needs.
Keep in mind

that I wish to lead you to the greatest joy in life.
Nothing has quite satisfied you altogether up to
     now,
even after trying everything.
Now we may come together to a port of endless
     joy.
The peace within you will grow slowly.
It will, though, eventually overflow from the
     Soul into the Body;
and by itself, it would be enough to sweeten hell.
Before this fully comes about, however,
much will have to be done.
Let the help of God's light comfort you.
Now, no more words, but deeds.

The Body answered:

You seem so intense as you come toward me that
     you frighten me.
You might commit some excess, make us both
     suffer.
I will do what you wish,
but first let me remind you of one thing.
The precept following that of loving God, you
     remember,
is that of loving our neighbor.
This love, in the temporal order,
begins with the love of your own body,
which you are to maintain alive and healthy
     under pain of sin.
You should not, therefore, endanger life or
     health.
Both are needed in order to come to what you
     seek, your end.
Life, quite simply, is a necessity.

When I, the Body, die,
you will have no means of adding to your glory,
nor any time for cleansing youself from your
    imperfections.
You will have to do that work in purgatory
—that is, suffer far more than you would in this
    world.
Nor can you do without your health.
When the body is healthy, the powers of the Soul
    are apt
to properly receive the light and inspiration of
    God;
and above all when joy overflows into the body.
When the body is sick, these powers are wanting.
You see, then, what is good for both of us.
In this way, each receives what is due him,
and both come to the port of salvation
without censure from heaven or earth.

The Soul replied:

Now I clearly see what I must do,
prompted by God's light and the voice of reason.
It is, however, a higher reason that I will listen
    to,
one that, hurting no one
and making it impossible for any to justly com-
    plain,
may grant to each his just needs.
No one, indeed,
who has submitted his appetites to higher reason
will find fault with what I will do.
Let me do as I will, then,
for you will lead a life far happier than you can
    possibly imagine.

In the beginning,
when I wanted to attend to the needs of the
   spirit,
I was in charge.
Through your deceit, you then bound yourself to
   me
and we agreed to do good together,
to have neither lord it over the other.
Gradually, however, you turned me into your
   slave.
Now I will once more be in charge.
If you wish to serve me, I will take care of all
   your needs;
if not, I will still be mistress and be served.
If needs be, I will compel you to be my servant—
and that will put an end to all arguments.

II

CONSIDERING man's sins, the Soul was astonished at the goodness of God, which, together with its own defects, it saw in a vision. And the Soul said:

O Lord, never more do I want to offend you,
or do anything against your goodness,
which has so bound me to you.
Nevermore will I stray from your command-
ments,
even though I were to suffer a thousand deaths.

Then turning toward her humanity [Human Frailty, the lower self] and seeing all its defects and bad instincts, the Soul said:

Do you think you are clean enough to appear in
the presence of God?
How do you look upon yourself?
Who will save you from your wretchedness?
Do you not see that you are not beautiful,
but are all splattered with mud?
You had hidden yourself with such subtle, cun-
ning self-love
that you thought that your sensuality was the
only paradise.
Now what is all this compared to God?
Nothing but the works of the devil.

I warn you, then, not to speak to me of unseemly
    things,
or I will make you pay for it.
I will treat you as a devil—that is, without
    respect.
Now that you see how much it matters not to
    offend God,
how can you say or think of anything
that has to do with your appetites?
And knowing all the while that it is against the
    will of God?
At any rate, do what you will,
I will not believe you any more than the devil.

On hearing these reproaches, Human Frailty hung its head and did not answer. The Soul, for its part, turning to God, said:

Lord, why did you illumine a soul so rank,
an enemy that constantly flees from you,
an obstinate, sensual soul?
Of what worth am I? I am vile!

Dwelling thus on itself, on what it would have come to had it followed its chosen road to the end, the Soul felt terror, and so did the Body. Moaning and crying out, the Soul said:

Wretched me, had I continued on that path,
the woes that would have been in store for me
in this world and in the next!

The suffering of the Soul was so great that it obliterated all other thoughts. Incapable of feeling any joy, the Soul seemed to be stifled in melancholy, completely at a loss as to what to do. Neither heaven nor earth offered it a place of rest, and it avoided the company of men and the remembrance of past joys or sadness.

I find myself responsible

The Soul said

for all the evil I have done
and I want to atone for it by myself.
Hell alone, I know, is the proper place for me,
but I can only go there after death.
Alas, my God, what shall I do with myself?
Where can I hide?
How can I appear in your presence sullied as I
am?
Still, I find you everywhere, and find myself
unbearable.
What am I to do with this filthy robe I wear?
Weeping does no good, nor sighing;
contrition is not acceptable and penance wins no
pardon,
for it cannot make satisfaction
for the punishment my sins deserve.

Unable to call out to the mercy of God, with no confidence in itself, the Soul nevertheless fought to ward off despair. Still, it suffered greatly, for it knew the weight it was carrying, the evil it had done; and in this distress the Soul [Catherine] was sick with heartache, unshed tears and sighs, sick unto death. She could not eat, sleep, or talk, nor had she any taste for things, either spiritual or earthly. She had no sense of where she was, in heaven or on earth, and would gladly have hidden from everyone. So alienated was she by the offense given to God that she looked more like a frightened animal than a human being. The pain of enduring that vision of sin was as keen-edged and hard as a diamond.

God, however, once He had her dwell on that vision, then provided for her in the following way.

One day there appeared to her inner vision Jesus Christ incarnate crucified, all bloody from head to foot. It seemed that the body rained blood. From within she heard a voice say, "Do you see this blood? It has been shed for your love, to atone for your sins." With that she received a wound of love that drew her to Jesus with such trust that it washed away all that previous fright, and she took joy in the Lord.

She was also granted another vision, more striking yet, beyond telling or imagination. God showed her the love with which He had suffered out of love of her. That vision made her turn away from every other love and joy that did not come directly from God.

In that vision, Catherine saw the evil in the soul and the purity of God's love. The two never left her. Had she dwelt on that vision any longer than she did, she would have fainted, become undone.

The vision made her dwell constantly on the evil of man, which could not have been greater, considering the great love of God, a love that never ceased doing the soul as much good as it could; and in turning her gaze upon herself, Catherine saw how much evil there was in her. That experience made her think of man in terms of the very opposite of the goodness of God, and this thought made her almost despair.

Had God not tempered this vision, body and soul would both have perished. But now Catherine became such an enemy of herself that when she had to use her name for one reason or another she preferred to say "we." She waged resolute war on the self-love that survived in her. Were an angel to have spoken well of her, she would not have believed him, so certain was she of the evil in her.

Because of that evil, which she felt to be irremediable, she almost despaired; still, trusting in God she said:

Lord, I make you a present of myself
I do not know what to do with myself.
Let me, then, Lord, make this exchange:
I will place this evil being into your hands.
You are the only one who can hide it in your
    goodness
and can so rule over me
that nothing will be seen of my own proper self.
On your part, you will grant your pure love,
which will extinguish all other loves in me
and will annihilate me and busy me so much
    with you
that I will have no time or place for anything or
    anyone else.

The Lord accepted. As a consequence, those preoccupations never troubled Catherine again. And with that exchange God sent her a ray of His love so burning and deep that it was an agony to sustain. Issuing from the fountain of Christ that love, wounding the soul, stripped it of all other loves, appetites, delights, and selfishness. The soul cried out, sighed deeply, and in its transformation was taken out of itself.

God deeply impressed upon her the fountains of Christ with their fiery bloody drops of love for man. He also impressed on her the vision of man, but limited the attendant suffering, so that at one and the same time she could endure both visions.

Armed with this love, she was sure of overcoming any obstacles or devils for she was in her fortress, God. Trusting in His goodness she could endure the sight of her lower self.

Thus, all that was not Pure Love meant nothing to her. She felt no attraction to any food that was not strictly necessary, nor to frequenting friends, even close ones.

She was very drawn to solitude, to God Himself alone; and God gave her the gift of prayer, so that she would be on her knees for six and seven hours. The uncomplaining body did all it could to help that soul drawn up by love. It could well be said of her, *Cor meum et caro mea exultaverunt in Deum vivum*, and her prayers were sighs, cries and inner fire.

God, who now ruled over her, took away the instinct for the things of the world and the self. He gave her other and better preferences. He made her moderate in her eating so that she stopped eating fruit (of which she was very fond) or meat or anything rich. So that she would still further lose the taste for eating, He had her use hepatic oil and ground agracio, with which she would season any food she had a particular liking for.

Now she looked constantly at the ground, never laughed or smiled or glanced at passersby. So absorbed was she that the outside seemed almost not to exist. Outwardly she seemed very unhappy but within her there was a great joy.

She tried to cut down on the hours of sleep by placing thorns under her, but still she continued to sleep, for God never took that away from her no matter how hard she tried.

Seeing that impetuosity of Spirit, the little concern shown for its interests, Human Frailty was very unhappy but did not dare speak out. Like a guilty thief who knows very well why he finds himself in prison, it cowered in fear of judgment, hoping only that things would eventually change. It was disappointed, however. The impetus of the Spirit did not diminish at all and the only rest Human Frailty got was when the Soul slept. Gradually it became like dry wood.

When asked by the Spirit how it fared, Human Frailty answered:

> I wonder how long you can keep up this pace.
> As for me, I look forward to death or sickness.
> May it come sooner than you think,
> so that not finding what you seek in this world
> you will go to purgatory,
> where in one moment alone you will suffer
> as you have here in a lifetime.
> I will be in the grave—
> not a bad place, all things considered,
> and much less demanding than living in this
>   world—
> but in purgatory you will be considerably worse
>   off.

The Spirit answered:

> I understand your plight,
> but as for me I hope neither for death nor for
>   suffering.
> Consider: The bad humors have almost been
>   purged away,
> and the diet has helped you.
> You're getting thin and pale.
> If no grain is in God's mill, the wheels go around
>   in vain.
> At any rate, I will offer you
> something other than death or sickness.

The Spirit by now was able to discern the smallest imperfection in it and act on that knowledge. It dealt with Human Frailty with dispatch and brooked no opposition. And Human Frailty said to itself:

> If I could only find some good
> in the things that nourish the Spirit,
> so that I too could get some benefit from all this.
> How else can I long endure this discipline, this
>   prison?

Lost in this thought, and finding itself in church, it received Communion and was so illumined that like the Soul it felt that it was already enjoying eternal bliss; and it cried out,

> Finally, I too feel alive!

At this point, though, the Soul (which strove after Pure Love) on hearing that cry protested and said,

> Lord, Lord, I want no signs from you
> nor am I looking for intense feelings to accompany your love.
> I would rather flee those feelings as I do the
>   devil.
> They get in the way of Pure Love—
> for under the guise of Pure Love
> it is those emotional feelings to which the soul
>   becomes attached.
> Love must be naked.
> I beseech you, therefore,
> to grant me no such additional feelings,
> for I do not care for them.

On hearing this, that the Spirit abhorred what it enjoyed and hoped to enjoy still more, Human Frailty, turning to the Spirit, said grumpily:

> You are not keeping your word.
> Without spiritual or bodily comforts, how can I
>   go on?

The Spirit answered:

> You think you are complaining with reason, but
>   listen to me.
> Though I told you that at the end we would
>   enjoy similar things,
> you still run after what pleases you, not what
>   makes you happy.
> Take joy in what gives me happiness, despise
>   what I despise.
> You are bent on holding on to your pleasures;
> but I will regulate them, indeed snuff them out.
> Acting as if you were sick,
> I will give you food fit for invalids,
> for the food you want would do you harm.
> You argue that spiritual pleasures come from
>   God
> and that therefore they can do only good.
> Do you not realize that in so arguing
> you show how sensuality clouds your intellect?
> Pure Love does not attach itself to pleasure or
>   feeling,
> bodily or spiritual.
> In the same way
> a spiritual attachment that seems good is danger-
>   ous:

It can mislead the Soul into attaching itself
not to God but to those pleasurable sentiments.
He who seeks the naked love of God must flee
   these sentiments.
Bodily sentiments, by contrast,
are obviously opposed to the Spirit
and the appearance of being good is not as
   persuasive—
that is why they are less dangerous.
Spiritual pleasures, however,
are something of a poison against pure love of
   God.
They are more difficult to eradicate once we
   become attached to them.
Not to understand this is to be barred from the
   one perfect good—
God pure and naked.
Now the peace I wish to give you,
which will give you joy, is still beyond your
   reach.
You are still too soiled.
First, then, I will clean the house and then
   furnish it
with those things that will give us not pleasure
   but joy.
I know that you say that you cannot endure as
   much;
I say you must.
What cannot be done in one year will be done in
   ten.
No doubt you will do all you can against me,
but rest assured that I will do the same.
Remember that in opposing you, I will do so to
   your advantage.
Do my will and in the end I will do yours.

Human Frailty answered:

> Consider my plight.
> Neither reason nor force is of much help
> in trying to escape from you.
> Answer me one question, though,
> and then I will patiently follow you as best I can.
> You who always speak about justice, take note.
> I am an animal body, without reason, power,
>   will, or memory.
> These are the attributes of the Spirit or Soul.
> I am no more than an instrument to be used as
>   you see fit.
> Any good or evil that I do, then, is your
>   responsibility.
> You were the one who sinned, in will and
>   intellect.
> I carried out your wishes.
> Tell me, then, who is it that deserves to be
>   punished?

The Spirit answered:

> These seem to be good objections, but I can deal
>   with them.
> If, as you maintain, you have never sinned,
> then God would not be just,
> since he wants the Body to go where the Soul
>   goes.
> This is a compelling argument.
> It must satisfy you.
> I confess, though,
> that I was the first to sin and to do so freely.
> The responsibility falls on me.
> In doing good, heaven and earth will come to my aid

and neither the devil, the flesh, nor the world
    can stand in the way.
If I commit evil,
then I too will have no shortage of those willing
    to help me—
demons, the world, the self, my instinct to evil.
God rewards good and punishes evil;
and those who do good will be rewarded.
You recall how it was in the beginning when we
    set out together.
I acted in keeping with my spiritual instincts
and did so with great intensity.
You objected vehemently.
We then turned to Self-Love to act as arbiter;
and he took sides sometimes with one,
sometimes with the other, and finished by
    corrupting both of us.
Should we both be punished,
in case (God forbid) of mortal sin,
of the two I would be the more severely
    punished,
although both of us no doubt would wish we had
    never been born.
Let us cleanse ourselves from all stain in this life,
then, from all bad habits.
I have been assured by God that before you leave
    me
there will be no stain whatsoever in us.
After all, how long can this purification last?
In the beginning it seemed unbearable,
but as bad habits disappear you will suffer less
    and less,
for God never allows man to carry a weight
that is greater than his strength.

How much better to suffer a little now than to
be in perpetual woe!

Having thus dealt with the objections and suffering of
Human Frailty, the Spirit left it and gave itself entirely to
Pure Love. It bound itself so tightly to it that Human
Frailty had barely room enough to breathe.

*   *   *

Ready and capable of enduring that love, the Soul was
now further tried by God, who infused such sweetness
into Catherine's heart that she was almost overwhelmed.

Love has eyes to see with, however, and this Soul
protested, insisting that it wanted no such proofs of love,
that they took away from love. I will protect myself, the
Soul asserted, as best I can against such sweetness, for
compared with Pure Love that is a poison. God, however,
paid no heed to her and maintained her in that fount of
love.

God also sent a ray of love so intense that had Self-
Love not tempered it, the Soul would have died. From
time to time God would show the Soul the self that
opposed pure love; and on contemplating it the Soul knew
that it would have preferred to die rather than to offend
God with any stain of sin.

Lost in Pure Love, the Spirit acted as if Human
Frailty no longer existed; and that lower self, which experienced how much more difficult things were becoming
day by day, said in a humble and respectful voice:

You have stripped me of all that can sustain me.
I might as well be dead.

The Spirit answered:

> The external goods I will grant you will give you
>   no pleasure.
> Indeed, you will despise them.

Human Frailty said:

> As long as something can be done,
> I will accept whatever you grant.
> Before I do anything,

the Spirit replied,

> I want you to experience obedience.
> In this way you will learn to be humble and
>   subject to others.

As a consequence Human Frailty was reduced to a pitiful
state. Had God not shown it mercy, it would not have
survived.

So that you will have something to do, God said to
her,

> you will work for a living.
> You [Catherine] will be asked to do works of
>   charity
> among the poor sick,
> and when asked you will clean filthy things.
> Should you be conversing with God at the time
> you will leave all and not ask who sends for you
>   or needs you.
> Do not do your will but that of others.
> You will have the time you need,
> for I intend to crush all disordered pleasures and
>   discipline you—

and I want to see results.
If I find that you consider some things repugnant
I will have you so concentrate on them
that they will no longer be such.
I will also take away
all those things that gave you some comfort
and make you die to them.
The better to test you,
I will have you endure a corresponding version
    in spiritual things
of those that give and take away pleasure.
You will have no friendships, no special family
    ties.
You will love everyone without love,
rich and poor, friends and relatives.
You are not to make friends,
not even spiritual or religious friendships,
or go to see anyone out of friendship.
It is enough that you go when you are called,
as I told you before.
This is the way you are to consort with your
    fellow creatures on earth.

And with that, one day the women in a confraternity of mercy asked Catherine for assistance, and she answered the call.

She found many who were horribly sick, full of lice and foul-smelling. Some of them, because of the intensity of their suffering, were desperate. Entering that place was like entering a tomb; but Catherine was determined to minister to the sick and give them some consolation, even those who cursed anyone who came to help them.

In addition to this work she also helped the poor in the hospital of San Lazzaro.

It seemed that the Spirit in these most trying tasks

was having her experience utter wretchedness. Her Human Frailty was beseiged on two sides—first, it found that wretchedness repugnant; and in addition it was suffering a terrible solitude, since the Spirit was so occupied with inner dialogue that it was cut off from external things.

Caught in this quandary, Human Frailty sought to escape but did not know how. It realized that the Spirit wanted it to work with human misery as if it were kneading bread, and even, if need be, to taste it a bit.

It was a pitiful sight to see this creature struggling so. Yet since those trials were a means of insuring the triumph of the Spirit, she overcame all obstacles.

The Spirit, having put Human Frailty to the test, then said to it:

Well, what do you think now?
I have shown you what we have to go through,
and you have tried the easy and the hard way.
Do what you will, with one proviso:
You will live among the sick in great humility
as long as I see fit and do so without interruption.

HUMAN FRAILTY

I have tried one extreme and the other.
Better to endure these trials than the fire of
   divine rays.
Still, one way and the other, both frighten me.

SPIRIT

When you have one, you will not have the other.
Let me warn you, though.
I intend to keep on living in this fashion,
pure and clean as at the moment of my creation.
I will go to any lengths to assure that.

HUMAN FRAILTY

Taking into account your resolve, my answer
  will be brief.
I put myself in your hands and hope for a
  speedy death.

*   *   *

Now to assure the annihilation of her Human Frailty,
since dealing with lice made Catherine almost vomit, the
Spirit said:

Take a handful of them,
put them in your mouth and swallow them.
That way you will free yourself of your nausea.

She shuddered but did as she was told, learning to handle
them as if they were pearls. Dealing with particularly big
lice was harder yet, but even then she obeyed. She did this
so often that she overcame that repugnance and nausea
once and for all.

The Spirit also showed her other sick persons with
foul-smelling sores, the stench of which was so great that
it was hard to stay close to them; and the Spirit had her
deal with those sores as she had dealt with the lice. She
put them into her mouth, and so many times that she was
freed from a natural repugnance; but since the smell
continued to give her nausea she rubbed her nose with the
pus until she freed herself of that revulsion.

In purely human terms, these loathesome actions
went contrary to human nature. Yet in forcing herself to
obey the Spirit, Catherine was heartened in her resolve to
help the desperately sick.

For three years the Spirit kept her absorbed in this
work, sustaining her within, so that she did these things
without taking much thought about them. After that he

put her to another test. She was asked to go to a hospital with her husband to serve the sick, and she was subject to those who ran the hospital as if she were a servant. She lived in one room with her husband. Though those who gave her the room admired her, no one showed much concern for her. She was not very talkative. When she was given a job to do she did it.

Empty of any support or refreshment within, completely alienated, Human Frailty said to the Spirit:

> If you want me to do this work, give me the
>   strength to do it.
> I will not shrink from anything,
> but to do this work well, love is needed.

Her wish was granted and she was given a certain corresponding love, but only when it was strictly necessary for the work.

She was left in these trials for many years before she was subjected to one further test.

To test her pride, the Spirit had her put in charge of the hospital. She was strengthened in her work by an increase of love, which had come about with a diminution of her human weakness. This love made her do all her work with dispatch so that she could then give herself completely to the divine fire of Pure Love. She spoke about this to no one.

She often spoke to herself, and small wonder; and just as the experience was known to her alone, so were the words. Who and what words could express the transformation of the self into spiritual being? The marvel is that she did not die from the fire of such love.

*　　*　　*

If the fire we know converts the consumed thing into itself, leaving nothing but ashes behind at the end, what shall we say of that essential fire whose strength flows from itself?

Catherine's soul, like the seraphim, had penetrated into essential fire, because of which she would cry out many times. She would often turn tenderly to animals and say "Aren't you, too, creatures of God?"—and all this she did because of the fire in her heart.

Though the Spirit now no longer considered her an ordinary human creature, since she was now without Human Frailty, nonetheless he subjected her to one last trial, to purify her still further. She died during this trial, the hardest one of all.

Nine years before her death she fell ill of an unknown sickness, one that baffled the doctors, for they did not realize that this sickness was the working of the Spirit. Medicine could not help. She suffered intolerably and many times appeared to be on the verge of death— and this lasted for a number of years.

Fires of love encircled her and many times it seemed as if she were about to die of them; especially in her last year when she ate in one week what a normal person would in a day.

To the last she always received the Eucharist. If she could not, that gave her more suffering than the illness. The day she did not receive Communion she was hungry all day long. It seemed that she could not live without the Sacrament.

III

TOWARD the end, four months before she died, she underwent one of the most profound experiences of her life. Many doctors were called in to visit her, to feel her pulse and to study the nature of her illness. It was their consensus that her malady was supernatural, that there was nothing they could do for her. The conclusion could be verified by observation, for there was no sign of bodily illness in her, as she correctly maintained for some time before, refusing the medicines that were constantly offered her.

"This illness of mine"

she would say,

"is not the type that is healed with medicines."

Yet since the doctors insisted, she would obediently take her medicine, though it was hard to take and did her no good. She continued to do so until the doctors realized their mistake.

It is hard to imagine what the Spirit had human weakness undergo—the suffering was so intense that those near her could barely endure the sight of that pain. Suffering broke that body from head to toe, so that there was no part of it that was not tormented by inner fire. There was also much internal bleeding.

134

She was not able to digest anything, though she ate very little and against her will, insisting that no bodily food was necessary. What pain it was for her to eat in those days! And the confirmation of what she said about her illness was that she remained without eating for fourteen days, something that in natural terms the body cannot do.

She never had trouble, however, in receiving Communion. They would bathe her lips with spring water, but she could not swallow it. Crying out in pain, she could never fall asleep at night. She felt herself burning within and without, and could not move of her own strength but had to be helped in all things.

And the Spirit took away all her friends and spiritual persons who were of help in her suffering, having them leave the room and leave her alone within and without.

She was tested in yet another way. She was allowed to have an overwhelming desire for some things, so strong that her human weakness would have given anything to obtain them. Once she had them, she found them tasteless and had to endure that sudden change, as if someone were toying with her.

Completely in charge of her person, the Spirit left her only the instinct for the Sacrament, which was never taken away from her. Utterly alone, within and without, besieged and seeking to draw herself together, she seemed nailed to the cross. Her suffering was beyond telling.

And yet, she experienced such joy and expressed it in such fiery words of love that all those who heard them wept. People came to visit her from great distances and all wondered and were edified in what they saw. They had, they were sure, seen someone more divine than human.

In the spirit of Catherine one saw paradise, and purgatory in her suffering body. The intensities of both were above the natural order.

And in her purified union with God and the fire she felt within, it was apparent that she had seen into the mirror of her spirit and humanity and had seen thereby the state of the souls in purgatory. That was why she spoke so well of the souls in purgatory, having herself been purified in the fire of divine love. O happy purgatory and happy soul who has passed through such glorious suffering!

Just as I am sure that after his martyrdom there was found written in St. Ignatius's body the word "Jesus," so I am equally certain that had anyone been able to look into her heart he would have found it burned by the fire of divine love.

For many years the outside of the body near the heart was as yellow as saffron. She would say that she felt the fire burn so fiercely that she marveled that she could remain alive—a sign that she was being consumed by the divine fire.

That this fire consumed not only the heart but also her human weakness, and through her many sufferings transformed her into something divine, was evident.

For after her death one could see, and this is still the case, the whole body turned as yellow as saffron, a sign that that divine fire had spread and consumed all of that humanity down to the last tiny particle.

Once her human frailty was consumed by fire, this blessed soul left that purgatory and flew to her sweet love.

Many doctors testified that her happy death, without any bodily illness, was something supernatural, a miracle; and considering her life, how her heart was pierced by divine love and how she spoke with God for many years, it does not seem unreasonable to believe what has been said of her here, for in no way does what has been said contradict the Christian faith. He who believes in this account does no wrong, and he who does not, does not offend.

This blessed soul experienced many graces in her last days. One day, no longer able to endure the fire of divine love, for the body felt as if it was about to dissolve, she turned to a picture of the Lord speaking to the Samaritan woman at the well and cried out,

"Lord, I beg of you,
give me a drop of that water
which you gave to the Samaritan woman,
for I can no longer endure this fire."

And her wish was granted. Tongue cannot tell the joy and freshness of the water He gave her.

She could never stay still for long, and needed frequent ministering, for because of that inner fire she was like someone almost dead.

On some days, though, it seemed that the body was quite healthy, and those present marveled at these changes, which reason could not explain. Clearly God helped her in secret.

One day she was shown the state of inner purity in which one must be found in order to find oneself in the presence of God after death without going through purgatory. And she was almost overcome when she saw how strait was the way, because then and there she realized that one had to be almost inhuman, something that was hard to grasp. She took this to mean that she had to lose her self and live like the dead, without taste or feeling. She saw that any part in her that could turn to created things had to be burned away.

Another day, she felt that she was up in the air and the spiritual part in her wanted to hold on to heaven and climb up together with the soul; the other part in her, the human part, would rather have attached itself to earth. It seemed that the two parts were struggling one against the other, but that neither could do much except remain in the air, neither attaching itself to what it sought, and both, because of that, felt sore distressed. After some time it seemed that the part striving toward heaven was winning and the human part, against its will, was also leaving earth far behind. At first the human part grieved. Once it could no longer see earth, it began to taste and enjoy heaven. In this way the two got along well together, and though on occasion the human part was nostalgic for earth, still that experience made it happier and happier. It slowly lost all its evil instincts and offered no more resistance to that part which wanted to make heaven its abode.

* * *

The soul, having been created pure and clean, has a certain natural instinct within it that makes it turn to God, and it cannot return to Him until it is once again pure and clean. Since it finds itself imprisoned in a heavy, corruptible body, which lacks this instinct, it waits with longing for its death and purification, much the same way that it feels when it leaves purgatory for paradise, for God makes a purgatory out of the body of some of its creatures.

The more God draws the soul up to Him, the more He instills in it the desire to be drawn up; once God has led the soul to the last step, when He wishes to release the soul and have it come home, the soul is so impatient to find itself in God that it experiences the body itself as purgatory.

Much the same way, the body with a soul that is very

diverse from it and very alien also feels that it is in purgatory.

The difference between the suffering of the body and of the soul, however, is as great as that between infinite good and infinite evil. The condition is one in which one is the master and the other is a servant. Were they both to be imprisoned, you can well imagine which would suffer most! There is no comparison between the finite and the infinite. There is nothing stronger than the instinct of the soul for God when nothing obstructs it, no force that can surpass it.

*　　*　　*

Another time, when Catherine was overcome again by love, to the Soul's great peace and joy, her Human Frailty, complaining, uttered these words:

"As for the spirit,
I sense such peace and joy that it goes beyond
    words;
with respect to humanity,
the deepest suffering a body can feel
is nothing to what I am experiencing."

Both Body and Soul waited to see the workings of God, which increased their joy and suffering. They did so patiently; and this was another sign that this Soul was in the furnace of burning love in which, as in purgatory, it was being purified.

Then the Soul was made to experience a spark of that Pure Love with which God had created it. That experience imparted such fire to her heart that all woes left her and she burned with a fire of that love which He had her experience. She so passionately answered that love that her heart was brimming over, utterly absorbed in that exchange, and the Soul came close to leaving the Body, leaving this earth and transforming itself into God. Whereupon her lower self, her humanity, said:

> You are endangering me to excess.
> I feel the roots that attach me to life cut,
> and find myself quite abandoned.
> All you do is concentrate on heaven and forget
> me.
> It seems to me that you seek to undo me with
> fiery arrows
> that pierce me to the quick.
> You make me cry out in pain,
> and would have me go scurrying about madly on
> all fours.

Her humanity cried out with a loud voice and no one paid heed. Those present concurred that no greater suffering was ever witnessed in a body to all appearances healthy. Seeing her immersed in such pain, those who were ministering to her and those devoted to her hoped for a speedy death.

*   *   *

She frequently had visions of angels and would laugh with them. They would see her laugh wordlessly, and then she would tell them she had seen angels.

This blessed soul walked the ways of God for some thirty-five years, with remarkable inner experiences, in a long succession of days, weeks, and months of a suffering that culminated in a happy death.

The night of the feast of St. Lawrence, it seemed that her body was on fire like that of the saint, for it thrashed about in all directions. On the following day, since her body was still in extreme pain, God visited her and drew her to Him. Catherine remained with her eyes fixed on the ceiling and did not move for an hour. Though she did not move or speak, she laughed with great joy.

When she came back to herself, she was asked what she had seen. She answered that God had shown her a spark of the joys of eternal life and that that had made her laugh out of sheer joy.

And all she said was:

"O Lord, do with me what You will."

This was a sign that she was approaching the end.

On August 14, the vigil of the feast of the Assumption, she was in great travail day and night, and it was thought that she was about to die. When she was about to receive Communion at the usual time, she spoke such loving words to the Sacrament that many present wept. In the presence of the Blessed Sacrament she was often passionately inspired, for her great and unutterable love for it penetrated to the deepest part of herself.

The subsequent day and night she was in great pain, and again many thought that she was about to die. She asked for Extreme Unction, which was given to her and which she received with great devotion.

The next day she was jubilant and laughed out loud. She thought she saw a divine face, which gave her immense joy. Those around her looked about but could not understand what made her so happy. When the vision disappeared she was asked what she had seen. She answered that she had seen extremely beautiful faces, happy and mirthful, and could not but rejoice with them.

This joy lasted for seven days, during which she seemed much improved, a truly supernatural phenomenon in the sudden passing from death to life.

On the vigil of St. Bartholomew, again as several times before, it seemed that she was about to die. She was twenty-four hours without food and if she took some she could not keep it on her stomach. At about seven o'clock in the evening she had a diabolical vision that assaulted her body and soul. Unable to speak, she motioned to them to make the sign of the cross above her heart, and she crossed herself, though it was difficult to make out what she was saying. Only later was it clear that she had been subjected to a diabolical temptation.

She beckoned to them to bring surplices, stoles, and holy water to her. This was done and in half an hour she felt liberated. Once more herself, she said that God had allowed her to be subjected to that temptation. And since she was so burning within with the fire of divine love, she felt such repugnance for that vision that she would gladly have hurled herself into hell rather than long endure that temptation. She was not shown sins she had ever committed, for that would have been much worse than the diabolical vision.

On the twenty-fifth of August she was so weak that she could barely keep her eyes open. She had them open the window so that she could see the sky. Later in the evening she had them light candles. As the candles were burning, she sang as well as she could the "Veni Creator Spiritus," and others accompanied her. When she had finished singing she looked up to heaven and remained thus for about an hour and a half. She moved her hands and eyes a great deal, which puzzled those standing by her, who wondered what she might be seeing, since she seemed so intensely happy that it appeared she would die of joy. When she came back to herself she said many times,

"Let us leave, let us leave."

And then she said,

"No more of this world, no more of this world."

The memory of that vision left her all broken so that she could neither speak nor move.

On the twenty-seventh of the month she saw herself without body and without soul, as she had always wished to be; that is, with her spirit completely in God, and having lost sight of heaven and earth, as if she no longer existed.

She saw this vision so clearly and felt so stripped down to her bare being that she had all leave her room and asked that only those who had to should come in. She had no dealings with any creature except out of pure necessity, nor did she want anyone to speak to her unless they had a compelling reason. She was so absorbed within that her humanity could not be concerned with any earthly thing. For two days she remained thus. It seemed as if she could find no rest and was quite out of herself.

On the next day, the twenty-eighth, she had a very hard day and night. Some four months before it seemed that on feast days, especially on those of the apostles, martyrs, and Our Lord, she felt more pain than on other days. Because of that inner fire she became as yellow as saffron, a sign that the inner fire was consuming her humanity.

On September 2 she seemed utterly without strength. She tried to take something, but it made matters worse, because of the efforts she had to make; and this happened several times. There was no way to help her.

She spoke only rarely, utterly drained of strength, burning with that inner fire without being able to drink as much as a drop of water. She easily swallowed the Communion wafer, however, and said that it was no sooner in her mouth than it was in her heart. Nor could she take any other food, for it would not stay down. At this point the doctors said that there was no point in forcing her to eat, that it only made matters worse, as she herself had insisted.

The following day, in great pain, she stretched out her arms so that she looked like a body nailed to the cross, her appearance reflecting her inner crucifixion. And she said:

> "Let every suffering and pain be welcome that
> comes from God's will,
> for you have illuminated me, O Lord,
> for the last thirty-six years or so.
> For your sake I have always sought to suffer,
> within as well as without.
> And this desire has never let me suffer greatly.
> On the contrary, all those things that I have
> undergone
> that seemed intense suffering
> were, because of your will, sweet and consoling.
> Now that I am at the end
> and seem to be in such pain from head to toe
> that it would seem that the body could not en-
> dure it
> and would be about to die and be quite
> annihilated,
> I see that you who rule over all things with your
> will
> do not want me to die as yet.
> So that in the midst of the pain my body en-
> dures,
> without comfort of any kind,
> I still cannot say that I am suffering.

You make all things bearable,
and my joy is such that it cannot be imagined or
   expressed."

As was her wont, on September 5 she received Communion. At the very moment she had a vision of a dead woman on a bier, accompanied by many religious dressed in black, and this vision gave her an immense joy; and she spoke of it to her confessor as if she had some scruples over such joy. The inner fire was intensifying and making her so weak that she could no longer move.

On September 6 a new nail was driven into her heart, which caused her great pain and lasted about ten hours. She would cry aloud, especially when she would abruptly wake from her sleep, which was not sleep, although it resembled it for she was so weak and exhausted that she seemed dead; and this happened because of the inner fire.

On September 7 she received Communion, observing the fast, without eating or drinking. In the twentieth hour she felt such joy that she could not but smile continuously for about two hours.

After this, she saw a ray of divine love that was almost unbearable and that burned up her humanity, which could not defend itself, given its frailty.

She then saw a ladder of flame and felt herself drawn upwards, experiencing great joy therein. This vision lasted for about four hours.

Because of the intense fire in which that humanity was being consumed, she asked those present to open the window to see whether the world was on fire. She was sure that was the case; and this showed that she was right in saying to her humanity that it would have been better off in a burning furnace than in that spiritual fire through which it had to pass to completely annihilate its nature.

On the eighth day of the month she received Communion in the usual way, remaining for all of those days without eating or drinking.

The following day she again received Communion in the same way. And in a vision she saw many of the wretched parts of her life, and that greatly distressed her. When she could speak of them she did, and then the distress left her. They were things of no importance, but for her the least defect was intolerable.

She then had the experience of a pure soul, incapable of any memory but those of things divine. And on contemplating this state she smiled and said,

"Oh, who could ever be worthy of all this!"

She so marveled at this vision that for a long time she seemed motionless and abstracted from all things.

A short time thereafter she saw another ray of divine fire, which gladdened her, but she could not express what she felt. Those near her, however, could tell that she was closer to heaven than to earth.

On the tenth she received Communion as usual, without having eaten or drunk, but the inner fire continued to rage.

In these days ten doctors gathered together to see whether they could help her in any way with their skills. On examining her, they concluded that her case was not a normal sickness but a supernatural one, for neither her pulse, urine, nor any other sign showed a bodily illness. And marveling, and asking her for her prayers, they left.

The fire was so intense that day that she felt she was reduced to ashes. If they put water in her mouth she would immediately spit it out and not a drop of it would be swallowed. All marveled at how she could continue to live without eating or drinking, and suffering so.

As for her clarity of mind, her speech, her pulse, all was normal (that is, when she was not so weak that she could not talk), but when she appeared to be suffocating she looked quite dead; and then abruptly she would come to again. This was evidently the working of God, and all marveled.

On the twelfth, she received Communion, as was customary. She remained for a while without talking and then, wetting her lips, she said,

"I am drowning!"

For a drop of water had gone down her throat and she could not swallow it. She did not talk or open her eyes for the rest of that day. At night, at the tenth hour, she complained of the fire and vomited some black clotted blood. There were also black blotches all over her body and in her weakness and suffering she could not recognize any of those who stood around her.

On the thirteenth, at the twenty-third hour, she vomited a great deal of blood, and that continued all night, so that she was extremely weak. At the usual hour she received Communion. On seeing the blood, so hot that basins in which it was gathered were burning, those present marveled that she could continue to live and felt that truly there was a fire in her. Then Catherine looked up at the ceiling, gesturing with her hands and trying to speak. Those present asked her what she wanted and she said,

"Drive away that beast, who wants to eat!"

and that was all they could make out.

On the fourteenth she again vomited much blood. Her pulse was barely audible, as fine as a hair, and often they could not find it. Nonetheless, she spoke clearly and strongly and that night, as usual, she received Communion.

She spent all of that day and the following night in the same condition until the sixth hour, at which time she was surrounded by many of her devoted followers, who witnessed all of these things.

She was then asked if she wanted to receive Communion. She answered by asking whether it was the usual time, and then pointed her finger toward heaven. The gesture implied that she was to receive Communion in heaven, where she would be perpetually united to that sweet Sacrament and her loving God.

Thus in that very hour, in all peace and tranquillity, she gently left this life and went to her sweet love, whom she now sees and takes joy in for all time. Until the very last she was clear in mind, and did not remain silent for more than a half hour.

Many devout people claimed to have seen her in the very moment that she died in the Lord, and the whole city felt a great devotion to her.

Her soul flew up to heaven, her body remained here with us. I do not think that any blood or bad humors were left in the body because of the abundance of blood that she vomited.

She also said to us, several months before her death, that when she was dead her heart should be opened up and it would be found to be charred by love. This was not done, because of certain so-called practical considerations.

And this happy death occurred on the fourteenth of September in 1510, at the sixth hour, a short time before she usually received Communion.

A vast crowd attended her funeral in the Church of the Hospital of Pammatone, and with great devotion and reverence she was placed in a new tomb, in which she remained for about eight months.

When the temporary tomb was opened to place her body in the newly erected monument, they found her intact from head to toe, with palpable flesh that on contact felt not as if it were consumed but rather dried out. A huge crowd was present to see this still intact body; and because of them and the crowds that followed it was necessary to leave that body exposed for eight days, in a chapel where it could be seen but not touched. The cloths in which the body had been wrapped were all rotted but the body was incorrupt; and this was taken to be a supernatural phenomenon. Many who called upon Catherine for graces were granted them. That holy body today is the object of popular devotion, given the saintly life of Catherine, the many graces granted to it in some thirty-five years, and the patience and incredible charity with which she sustained such long suffering.

Everyone marveled on seeing that body intact, as on the day of burial, with no odor save some mustiness, and with no worms. Around the heart and above it the skin was red, a sign of the love it had borne. The rest of the body was yellow.

It is already ten years that the body continues in this integrity in a marble tomb, on high, in a wooden box, in the church mentioned above. Many people have a great devotion to Catherine and many prayers have been granted, and devotion to her is increasing, especially among those who knew her.

He who has seen these works for fifteen years and had a close knowledge of her as well as one of more ordinary relationships is convinced that everything that is written and said about her is as nothing compared with the truth.

And he who has seen these things and then written of them has been tempted to tear them all up, for it seemed to him that those poor little words could give no idea of Catherine.

But God has let these words be written and preserved for some illuminated people in particular.

Most beloved daughter, I have finished writing down the above work for you. I think there are many mistakes in it that are my fault, for I do not know how to write nor to do much well; and so you will forgive me if you find some errors in the writing. In composing this I have written as I have found. One thing I will tell you, that never did I labor as much over anything I put down on paper. Please say a prayer for the author.

April 20, 1671, Genova. This book of Blessed Catarineta Adorna has been copied from another old manuscript given by Sister ... , Rector of the Great Hospital, who says that she received it from the sisters of the Madonna delle Grazie. It is extremely probable that it is the manuscript copied by Ettore Vernazza and sent to V. D. Battistina, his daughter. This book, given the age of the paper, the print, the binding and other details, has been judged by experts to belong to that period. In testimony thereof,

Jo. P. Angelo Luigi Giovo, Protonotary

SELECTED BIBLIOGRAPHY

Two works tower in the bibliography on Catherine of Genoa: von Hügel's *The Mystical Element of Religion as Studied in Saint Catherine of Genoa and Her Friends* (London, 1908) and the two-volume work of Padre Umile Bonzi da Genova, *S. Caterina da Genova* (Marietti, 1960–1962). Their virtues are of a different order. The scholarship of Padre Umile is in some respects superior. This advantage, however, does not substantially detract from von Hügel's study. That work continues to be seminal.

Among other works that can be consulted with profit, many of which include bibliographies of their own, we should like to mention:

Bonzi da Genova, P. Umile. "La teologia purgatoriale di S. Bonaventura e quella di S. Caterina da Genova comparate." In *Vita Cateriniana*, nos. 3–13.

Castiglioni Humani, M. *S. Caterina da Genova*. Bari, 1960.

Cervetto, L. A. *Santa Caterina Fieschi Adorno e i Genovesi*. Genoa, 1910.

Debongnie, P. *Sainte Catherine de Gênes*. Bruges, 1959.

Da Pantasina, Gabriele. *S. Caterina da Genova*. Genoa, 1929.

Hello, E. *Profili di Santi: S. Caterina da Genova*. Florence, 1930.

Teodosio da Voltri. *S. Caterina da Genova, la gran Dama dell'Amore*. Genoa, 1929.

Trucco, F. *Il Purgatorio e la vita delle anime purganti secondo S. Caterina da Genova*. Prato, 1915.

Among works of a more general nature:

Bargellini, M. *Storia popolare di Genova dalla sua origine sino ai nostri tempi*. Genoa, 1856.

Baruzi, I. *St. Jean de la Croix et l'expérience mystique*. Paris, 1924.

Bianconi, A. *L'opera della Congregazione del Divino Amore nella Riforma cattolica*. Città di Castello, 1914.

Da Langasco, Cassiano. *Gli Ospedali degli Incurabili*. Genoa, 1938.

———.*Pammatone, cinque secoli di vita ospedaliera*. Genoa, 1953.

Dictionnaire de Spiritualité. Paris, 1937.

Donaver, F. *La storia della Repubblica di Genova*. Genoa, 1913.

Farina, John. "Nineteenth Century American Interest in Catherine of Genoa. "Unpublished manuscript, 1978.

Olin, John. *The Catholic Reformation—From Savonarola to Ignatius Loyola*. New York: Harper & Row, 1969.

Parodi, F. M. *La Compagnia del Mandiletto in Genova*. La Spezia, 1901.

Paschini, P. *La beneficenza in Italia e le Compagnie del Divino Amore nei primi decenni del Clinquecento*. Rome, 1925.

Underhill, E. *Mysticism*. New York: E. P. Dutton, 1961.

——.*The Mystics of the Church*. New York: Schocken, 1964.

Wapnick, Kenneth. "Mysticism and Schizophrenia." *Journal of Transpersonal Psychology 6*, no. 1, 1972.

Translations

English:

Manning Henry Cardinal. Introduction. *Treatise on Purgatory*, anonymous translation.

Ripley, Mrs. G. *Life and Doctrine of Saint Catherine of Genoa*, preface by Isaac Hecker. New York: Christian Press Association Publishing Co., 1896.

Balfour, Charlotte, and Irvine, Helen Douglas. *Treatise on Purgatory*. London: Sheed and Ward, 1946.

Upham, Thomas Coswell. *Life of Madam Catharina Adorna*. New York: Harper, 1858.

Spanish:

Barcelona, Antonio M. de. *Tratado del Purgatorio de Santa Catalina de Génova*. Barcelona, 1939.

Bergamin, J. *Tratado del Purgatorio de Santa Catalina de Génova*. Mexico, 1941.

French:

Traité du Purgatoire. Vie Spirituelle, S. Maximin, 1922.

Debongnie, P. *La grande dame du pur amour, Sainte Catherine de Gênes*. Études Carmelitaines, Bruges, 1959.

De Bussierre, M. T. *Les Oeuvres de Sainte Catherine de Gênes*. Paris, 1913.

German:

Sertorius, L. *Katharina von Genua, Lebensbilde und geistige Gestalt, Ihre Werke*. Munich, 1939.

INDEXES

Index to Introduction
and Notes on Translation

157

Faber, F.W., 42.
Falconieri, Juliana, 19.
Farina, John, 2, 39, 40.
Fénelon, 1, 39, 40.
Ficino, Marsilio, 24, 64.
Fieschi, Giacomo (father of Catherine), 2.
Fieschi, Giacomo (brother of Catherine), 3.
Fieschi, Napoleone, 3.
Fieschi, Roberto, 3.
Fieschi, Tommasina (Tommasa), 8, 23, 24.
Fioretti, 51.
Francis de Sales, 1, 29, 38.
St. Francis of Assisi, 4, 33, 51, 61, 65, 66.
Francis Xavier, 43.
Freedom, 26, 29, 30.
Freemantle, Anne, 43.
Freud, S., 22.

Geneti, Jacobo, 20.
Geronimo of Genoa, 20.
Giovo, Angelo Luigi, 52.
God, children of, 28; experience of, 20; gifts of, 17, 18; goodness of, 33; image of, 29; justice of, 34; love for, 3, 16, 17, 28, 32, 34, 40; love of, 18, 27, 28, 33, 35, 36, 42, 47, 54, 59, 66; mercy of, 4, 27, 34; nature of, 24, 31; surrender to, 26; trust in, 33, 38; union with, 18, 30, 31, 34-36, 40, 65; will of, 5, 17, 18, 34-36, 40.
Gonzaga, Aloysius, 38.
Grace, 33, 65.
Gregory of Nyssa, 31.
Groeschel, B., 64.
Guyon, Madame, 39.

Hard Sayings, 42.
Hecker, Isaac, 2, 40, 41.
Hell, 34, 43.

Henry VII, 18.
Hesse, Herman, 21.
Holy Spirit, 39, 41.
l'Homme religieu, 39.
Hours at Home, 40.
Hügel, F., von, passim 2-39; and manuscripts, 50-59.
Human Frailty, 22, 25, 26, 29.
Humanity, in *Spiritual Dialogue*, 49, 58.
Huxley, Aldous, 11.

Innocent IV, 3.
Innocent XI, 20.
Intellect, 29.
Irvine, Helen Douglas, 50.
Isaiah, 23.

Jacopone da Todi, 23, 24, 27, 29, 62, 63.
John, 23, 28; 14:9, 30; 14:23, 30; 17:23-24, 30.
John of the Cross, 29, 38.
The Journey of the Soul to God, 29.
Joy, 61, 64, 65.
Jung, C.G., 12, 23, 31.

Ladies of Mercy, 13.
Leo X, 47.
Love, for God, 3, 16, 17, 28, 32, 34, 40; of God, 18, 27, 28, 33, 35, 36, 42, 47, 54, 59, 66; for nature, 17; Pure Love, 14, 27, 28, 29, 32, 33, 35, 36, 38, 43, 59, 66.
The Life and Doctrine of St. Catherine of Genoa, 40.
Lutheranism, 47.

Madonna delle Grazie, see Santa Maria Delle Grazie.
Man, creation of, 31.
Manning, Henry Cardinal, 1, 42, 50.
Marabotto, Dom Cattaneo, 6, 16, 17, 20, 22, 57, 59, 60, 61, 67.

Index to Texts

Adam, 108.
Assumption, 141.

Baptism, 80.
St. Bartholomew, 142.
Body, appetites of, 101, 103, 104, 106, 113; as bonds of soul, 86, 114, 138; harm to, 96; needs of, 96-104, 106, 110, 111, 113, 114; salvation of, 96, 113; subject to soul, 91, 111, 114, 125, 139; suffering of, 139, 140; united to soul, 93, 103, 112, 113; and world, 92, 95, 97, 98, 101, 102.

Catherine, cf. Visions; body of, 149; and confession, 109; death of, 136, 148; and despair, 118, 119; dying of, 134-148; and Eucharist, 110, 133, 135, 141; life of, 120, 127-132; and love, 108-110, 118, 129, 135, 139; purification of, 133, 136; and sin, 108, 109, 117, 118, 142; suffering of, 118, 119, 133, 135, 143-146, 149; testing of, 127, 132, 133, 135, 142.
Charity, 71, 72, 96, 105, 128.
Christ, ascension of, 108; blood of, 84; crucified, 118; incarnation of, 108; love of, 108, 119; vision of, 118.
Contrition, 82, 84, 117.

Death, of body, 113; of Catherine, 136, 148; eternal, 110; fear of, 103; longing for, 138; and soul, 108, 115.
Devil, 115, 116, 120, 122, 126.

Eucharist, 110, 133, 135, 141, 143, 145-148; and joy, 122; love for, 141.

Evil, 74, 80, 83, 108, 109, 117-119, 126.
Extreme Unction, 141.

Fire, of divine rays, 130, 132, 133, 146; inner, 134, 136, 137, 143, 145-147; of love, 133, 136, 137, 139, 142.
Forgiveness, of debt, 82; denied, 74, 82; and sorrow, 75.

God, Being of, 86; essence of, 78; experience of, 71, 86, 106, 109; gifts of, 94, 107, 120; glory of, 78; goodness of, 71, 73-75, 78, 83, 86, 106, 109, 115, 118-120; help of, 97, 107, 110, 112; honor to, 87, 99; instinct for, 73, 74, 76, 85, 106, 126, 139; as judge, 126; justice of, 75, 77, 82-84, 86, 125; knowlege of, 86, 87, 102; light of, 72, 83, 87, 112, 113; love for, 78, 100, 108, 112, 139, 140; love of, 71-73, 77-81, 84, 86, 108-110, 118, 119, 122, 124, 136; mercy of, 71, 75, 77, 78, 83, 84, 86, 109, 117, 128; offending of, 87, 93-96, 109, 115-117, 127; ordinance of, 77, 82, 84, 86, 87, 103; presence of, 71, 78, 83, 86, 109, 115, 117, 137; trust in, 107, 109, 120; turning to, 105, 107, 116, 120, 124, 138; union with, 71, 72, 76, 80, 81, 86, 87, 110, 115, 136, 148; will of, 71, 72, 75-77, 79, 82, 83, 108, 110, 116, 141, 144; workings of, 80, 81, 86, 95, 139, 147.
Grace, 72, 78, 81, 84, 86, 107, 137, 149.
Guilt, 74.

Hell, 74, 76, 82, 84, 105, 109, 112, 117.

162

tion, 94, 99, 127, 146; creation of, 73, 75, 77-82, 91, 94, 102, 107, 108, 130, 138, 139; debt of, 82, 83; and despair, 117; and emotions, 122, 124, 127; end of, 76, 77, 82, 86, 99; enemies of, 107, 110; and God, 73, 77-81, 84, 86, 87, 115; harm to, 96-98; illumination of, 107, 108, 111, 116, 144; instinct for God in, 73, 74, 76, 85, 106, 126, 139; nature of, 92, 94, 103, 106, 125; needs of, 91, 97, 98, 100, 103-105, 114; perfection of, 79-82; purification of, 71, 75, 77, 79, 80, 82, 113, 138, 139; rest (peace) of, 77, 80, 86, 94, 103, 105, 111, 117, 139, 148; salvation of, 96, 103, 107, 113; shame of, 106; testing of, 127; transformation of, 81, 83, 103, 109, 119, 136, 140; voyage of, 91, 99; weakened, 100, 102, 106, 114; and world, 103, 105; worthiness of, 94, 116, 146.

Spirit, annihilation of, 131, 133; and evil, 126; and Human Frailty, 120, 122-124, 127, 129, 134, 135; impetus of, 121; will of, 124.

Suffering, duration of, 72, 74, 75, 82, 109; in hell, 74, 75; for love, 118; in purgatory, 71, 72, 74, 75, 77-79, 82, 84, 85, 87, 113, 121; and sin, 71, 73, 84, 126, 127; of soul, 116, 117, 139; willingness for, 84

Veni Creator Spiritus, 142
Vernazza, Battistina, 150
Vernazza, Ettore, 150.
Visions (of Catherine), of angels, 140; of Christ, 118; diabolical, 142; of eternal life, 141; of God, 84, 85, 109, 115, 118, 143; of joy, 141, 142, 145; of ladder of flame, 145; of love, 109, 118, 145; of man, 119; of sin, 73, 118, 146; of soul, 86, 108, 137.

Will, 87; alienated, 85; creation of, 98; evil, 74; freedom of, 74, 93, 98; of God, 71, 72, 75-77, 79, 82, 83, 108, 110, 116, 141, 144; and sin, 125; of soul, 98, 124; of soul in purgatory, 75, 77, 82.